SO-AFN-106

/. 00

A LITERARY CHRISTMAS

CONTENTS

BEFORE CHRISTMAS

THE NATIVITY

CHRISTMAS DAY

CHRISTMAS FARE

CHRISTMAS AT WAR

BEFORE CHRISTMAS

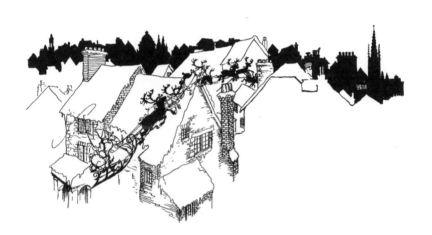

CLEMENT CLARKE MOORE

A Visit from St Nicholas

'Twas the night before Christmas, when all through the house
Not a creature was stirring, not even a mouse;
The stockings were hung by the chimney with care,
In hopes that St Nicholas soon would be there;
The children were nestled all snug in their beds,
While visions of sugar-plums danced in their heads;
And mamma in her 'kerchief, and I in my cap,
Had just settled our brains for a long winter's nap;
When out on the lawn there arose such a clatter,
I sprang from the bed to see what was the matter.
Away to the window I flew like a flash,
Tore open the shutters and threw up the sash.
The moon on the breast of the new-fallen snow,
Gave the lustre of mid-day to objects below,
When, what to my wondering eyes should appear,
But a miniature sleigh, and eight tiny reindeer
With a little old driver, so lively and quick,
I knew in a moment it must be St Nick.
More rapid than eagles his coursers they came,
And he whistled, and shouted, and called them by name;
'Now *Dasher*! now, *Dancer*! now, *Prancer* and *Vixen*!
On, *Comet*! on, *Cupid*! on, on *Donner* and *Blitzen*!
To the top of the porch! to the top of the wall!
Now dash away! dash away! dash away all!'
As dry leaves that before the wild hurricane fly,

When they meet with an obstacle, mount to the sky;
So up to the house-top the coursers they flew,
With the sleigh full of Toys, and St Nicholas too.
And then, in a twinkling, I heard on the roof,
The prancing and pawing of each little hoof.
As I drew in my head, and was turning around,
Down the chimney St Nicholas came with a bound.
He was dressed all in fur, from his head to his foot,
And his clothes were all tarnished with ashes and soot;
A bundle of Toys he had flung on his back,
And he looked like a peddler, just opening his pack.
His eyes – how they twinkled! his dimples how merry!
His cheeks were like roses, his nose like a cherry!
His droll little mouth was drawn up like a bow,
And the beard of his chin was as white as the snow;
The stump of a pipe he held tight in his teeth,
And the smoke it encircled his head like a wreath;
He had a broad face and a little round belly,
That shook when he laughed, like a bowlful of jelly.
He was chubby and plump, a right jolly old elf,
And I laughed when I saw him, in spite of myself;
A wink of his eye and a twist of his head,
Soon gave me to know I had nothing to dread;
He spoke not a word, but went straight to his work,
And fill'd all the stockings, then turned with a jerk,
And laying his finger aside of his nose,
And giving a nod, up the chimney he rose;
He sprang to his sleigh, to his team gave a whistle,
And away they all flew like the down of a thistle.
But I heard him exclaim, ere he drove out of sight,
"Happy Christmas to all, and to all a good night."

Arnold Bennett

from *The Feast of St Friend*

If then, there is to be a festival, why should it not be the festival of Christmas? It can, indeed, be no other. Christmas is most plainly indicated. It is dignified and made precious by traditions which go back much further than the Christian era; and it has this tremendous advantage – it exists! In spite of our declining faith, it has been preserved to us, and here it is, ready to hand. Not merely does it fall at the point which uncounted generations have agreed to consider as the turn of the solar year and as the rebirth of hope! It falls also immediately before the end of the calendar year, and thus prepares us for a fresh beginning that shall put the old to shame. It could not be better timed. Further, its traditional spirit of peace and goodwill is the very spirit which we desire to foster. And finally its customs – or at any rate, its main customs – are well designed to symbolize that spirit. If we have allowed the despatch of Christmas cards to degenerate into naught but a tedious shuffling of paste-boards and overwork of post-office officials, the fault is not in the custom but in ourselves. The custom is a most striking one – so long as we have sufficient imagination to remember vividly that we are all in the same boat – I mean, on the same planet, and clinging desperately to the flying ball, and dependent for daily happiness on one another's good will! A Christmas card sent by one human being to another human being is more than a piece of coloured stationery sent by one log of wood to another log of wood: it is an inspiring and reassuring message of high value. The mischief is that so many self-styled human beings are just logs of wood, rather stylishly dressed...

Edward Thomas

The Gypsy

A fortnight before Christmas Gypsies were everywhere:
Vans were drawn up on wastes, women trailed to the fair.
'My gentleman,' said one, 'You've got a lucky face.'
'And you've a luckier,' I thought, 'if such a grace
And impudence in rags are lucky.' 'Give a penny
For the poor baby's sake.' 'Indeed I have not any
Unless you can give change for a sovereign, my dear.'
'Then just half a pipeful of tobacco can you spare?'
I gave it. With that much victory she laughed content.
I should have given more, but off and away she went
With her baby and her pink sham flowers to rejoin
The rest before I could translate to its proper coin
Gratitude for her grace. And I paid nothing then,
As I pay nothing now with the dipping of my pen
For her brother's music when he drummed the tambourine
And stamped his feet, which made the workmen passing grin,
While his mouth-organ changed to a rascally Bacchanal dance
'Over the hills and far away'. This and his glance
Outlasted all the fair, farmer and auctioneer,
Cheap-jack, balloon-man, drover with crooked stick, and steer,
Pig, turkey, goose, and duck, Christmas Corpses to be.
Not even the kneeling ox had eyes like the Romany.
That night he peopled for me the hollow wooded land,
More dark and wild than stormiest heavens, that I searched and
  scanned

Like a ghost new-arrived. The gradations of the dark
Were like an underworld of death, but for the spark
In the Gypsy boy's black eyes as he played and stamped his
    tune,
'Over the hills and far away', and a crescent moon.

D.H. Lawrence

from *Sons and Lovers*

He was coming at Christmas for five days. There had never been such preparations. Paul and Arthur scoured the land for holly and evergreens. Annie made the pretty paper hoops in the old-fashioned way. And there was unheard-of extravagance in the larder. Mrs Morel made a big and magnificent cake. Then, feeling queenly, she showed Paul how to blanch almonds. He skinned the long nuts reverently, counting them all, to see not one was lost. It was said that eggs whisked better in a cold place. So the boy stood in the scullery, where the temperature was nearly at freezing-point, and whisked and whisked, and flew in excitement to his mother as the white of egg grew stiffer and more snowy.

'Just look, mother! Isn't it lovely?'

And he balanced a bit on his nose, then blew it in the air.

'Now, don't waste it,' said the mother.

Everybody was mad with excitement. William was coming on Christmas Eve. Mrs Morel surveyed her pantry. There was a big plum cake, and a rice cake, jam tarts, lemon tarts, and mince-pies – two enormous dishes. She was finishing cooking – Spanish tarts and cheese-cakes. Everywhere was decorated. The kissing bunch of berried holly hung with bright and glittering things, spun slowly over Mrs Morel's head as she trimmed her little tarts in the kitchen. A great fire roared. There was a scent of cooked pastry. He was due at seven o'clock, but he would be late. The three children had gone to meet him. She was alone. But at a quarter to seven Morel came in again. Neither wife nor husband spoke. He sat in his arm-chair, quite awkward with excitement, and she quietly went on with her baking. Only by the careful way in which she did things could it be told how much moved she was. The clock ticked on.

'What time dost say he's coming?' Morel asked for the fifth time.

'The train gets in at half past six,' she replied, emphatically.

'Then he'll be here at ten past seven.'

'Eh, bless you, it'll be hours late on the Midland,' she said, indifferently. But she hoped, by expecting him late, to bring him early. Morel went down the entry to look for him. Then he came back.

'Goodness, man!' she said. 'You're like an ill-sitting hen.'

'Hadna you better be gettin' him summat t'eat ready?' asked the father.

'There's plenty of time,' she answered.

'There's not so much as *I* can see on,' he answered, turning crossly in his chair. She began to clear her table. The kettle was singing. They waited and waited.

Meantime the three children were on the platform at Sethley Bridge, on the Midland main line, two miles from home. They waited one hour. A train came – he was not there. Down the line the red and green lights shone. It was very dark and very cold.

'Ask him if the London train's come,' said Paul to Annie, when they saw a man in a tip cap.

'I'm not,' said Annie. 'You be quiet – he might send us off.'

But Paul was dying for the man to know they were expecting someone by the London train: it sounded so grand. Yet he was much too much scared of broaching any man, let alone one in a peaked cap, to dare to ask. The three children could scarcely go into the waiting-room, for fear of being sent away, and for fear something should happen whilst they were off the platform. Still they waited in the dark and cold.

'It's an hour an' a half late,' said Arthur pathetically.

'Well,' said Annie, 'it's Christmas Eve.'

They all grew silent. He wasn't coming. They looked down the darkness of the railway. There was London! It seemed the utter-most of distance. They thought anything might happen if one came from London. They were all too troubled to talk. Cold, and unhappy, and silent, they huddled together on the platform.

At last, after more than two hours, they saw the lights of an engine peering round, away down the darkness. A porter ran out. The children drew back with beating hearts. A great train, bound for Manchester, drew up. Two doors opened, and from one of them, William. They flew to him. He handed parcels to them cheerily, and immediately began to explain that this great train had stopped for *his* sake at such a small station as Sethley Bridge: it was not booked to stop.

Meanwhile, the parents were getting anxious. The table was set, the chop was cooked, everything was ready. Mrs Morel put on her black apron. She was wearing her best dress. Then she sat, pretending to read. The minutes were a torture to her.

'H'm!' said Morel. 'It's an hour an' a ha'ef.'

'And those children waiting!' she said.

'Th' train canna ha' come in yet,' he said.

'I tell you, on Christmas Eve they're *hours* wrong.'

They were both a bit cross with each other, so gnawed with anxiety. The ash tree moaned outside in a cold, raw wind. And all that space of night from London home! Mrs Morel suffered.

The slight click of the works inside the clock irritated her: it was getting so late; it was getting unbearable.

At last there was a sound of voices, and a footstep in the entry.

'Ha's here!' cried Morel, jumping up.

Then he stood back. The mother ran a few steps towards the door and waited. There was a rush and a patter of feet, the door burst open, William was there. He dropped his Gladstone bag and took his mother in his arms.

'Mater!' he said.

'My boy!' she cried.

And for two seconds, no longer, she clasped him and kissed him. Then she withdrew and said, trying to be quite normal:

'But how late you are!'

'Aren't I!' he cried, turning to his father. 'Well, dad!'

The two men shook hands.

'Well, my lad!'

Morel's eyes were wet.

'We thought tha'd niver be commin',' he said.

'Oh, I'd come!' exclaimed William.

Then the son turned round to his mother.

'But you look well,' she said proudly, laughing.

'Well!' he exclaimed. 'I should think so – coming home!'

He was a fine fellow, big, straight, and fearless-looking. He looked round, at the evergreens and the kissing bunch, and the little tarts that lay in their tins on the hearth.

'By jove! mother, it's not different!' he said, as if in relief.

Everybody was still for a second. Then he suddenly sprang forward, picked a tart from the hearth, and pushed it whole into his mouth.

'Well, did iver you see such a parish oven!' the father exclaimed.

He had brought them endless presents. Every penny he had, he had spent on them. There was a sense of luxury overflowing in the house. For his mother there was an umbrella with gold on the pale handle. She kept it to her dying day, and would have lost anything rather than that. Everybody had something gorgeous, and besides, there were pounds of unknown sweets: Turkish delight, crystallised pineapple, and such like things which, the children thought, only the splendour of London could provide. And Paul boasted of these sweets among his friends.

'Real pineapple, cut off in slices, and then turned into crystal – fair grand!'

Everybody was mad with happiness in the family. Home was home, and they loved it with a passion of love, whatever the suffering had been. There were parties, there were rejoicings. People came in to see William, to see what difference London had made to him. And they all found him 'such a gentleman, and *such* a fine fellow, my word!'

Laurie Lee

from *Cider with Rosie*

THE WEEK before Christmas, when the snow seemed to lie thickest, was the moment for carol-singing; and when I think back to those nights it is to the crunch of snow and to the lights of the lanterns on it. Carol-singing in my village was a special tithe for the boys, the girls had little to do with it. Like hay-making, blackberrying, stone-clearing and wishing-people-a-happy-Easter, it was one of our seasonal perks.

By instinct we knew just when to begin it; a day too soon and we should have been unwelcome, a day too late and we should have received lean looks from people whose bounty was already exhausted. When the true moment came, exactly balanced, we recognised it and were ready.

So as soon as the wood had been stacked in the oven to dry for the morning fire, we put on our scarves and went out through the streets, calling loudly between our hands, till the various boys who knew the signal ran out from their houses to join us.

One by one they came stumbling over the snow, swinging their lanterns around their heads, shouting and coughing horribly.

'Coming carol-barking then?'

We were the Church Choir, so no answer was necessary. For a year we had praised the Lord, out of key, and as a reward for this service – on top of the Outing – we now had the right to visit all the big houses, to sing our carols and collect our tribute.

Eight of us set out that night. There was Sixpence the Tanner,

13

who had never sung in his life (he just worked his mouth in church); the brothers Horace and Boney, who were always fighting everybody and always getting the worst of it; Clergy Green, the preaching maniac; Walt the bully, and my two brothers. As we went down the lane, other boys, from other villages, were already about the hills, bawling 'Kingwenslush', and shouting through keyholes 'Knock on the knocker! Ring at the Bell! Give us a penny for singing so well!' They weren't an approved charity as we were, the Choir; but competition was in the air.

Our first call as usual was the house of the Squire, and we trooped nervously down his drive. For light we had candles in marmalade-jars suspended on loops of string, and they threw pale gleams on the towering snowdrifts that stood on each side of the drive. A blizzard was blowing, but we were well wrapped up, with Army puttees on our legs, woollen hats on our heads, and several scarves around our ears.

As we approached the Big House across its white silent lawns, we too grew respectfully silent. The lake near by was stiff and black, the waterfall frozen and still. We arranged ourselves shuffling around the big front door, then knocked and announced the Choir.

A maid bore the tidings of our arrival away into the echoing distances of the house, and while we waited we cleared our throats noisily. Then she came back, and the door was left ajar for us, and we were bidden to begin. We brought no music, the carols were in our heads. 'Let's give 'em "Wild Shepherds",' said Jack. We began in confusion, plunging into a wreckage of keys, of different words and tempo; but we gathered our strength; he who sang loudest took the rest of us with him, and the carol took shape if not sweetness.

This huge stone house, with its ivied walls, was always a mystery to us. What were those gables, those rooms and attics, those narrow windows veiled by the cedar trees? As we sang 'Wild Shepherds' we craned our necks aping into that lamplit hall which we had never entered; staring at the muskets and untenanted chairs, the great tapestries furred by dust – until suddenly, on the stairs, we saw the old Squire himself standing and listening with his head on one side.

He didn't move until we'd finished; then slowly he tottered towards us, dropped two coins in our box with a trembling hand, scratched his name in the book we carried, gave us each a long look with his moist blind eyes, then turned away in silence.

As though released from a spell, we took a few sedate steps, then broke into a run for the gate. We didn't stop till we were out of the grounds. Impatient, at least, to discover the extent of his bounty, we squatted by the cowsheds, held our lanterns over the book, and saw that he had written 'Two Shillings'. This was quite a good start. No one of any worth in the district would dare to give us less than the Squire.

So with money in the box, we pushed on up the valley, pouring scorn on each other's performance. Confident now, we began to consider our quality and whether one carol was not better suited to us than another. Horace, Walt said, shouldn't sing at all; his voice was beginning to break. Horace disputed this and there was a brief token battle – they fought as they walked, kicking up divots of snow, then they forgot it, and Horace still sang.

Steadily we worked through the length of the valley, going from house to house, visiting the lesser and the greater gentry – the farmers, the doctors, the merchants, the majors and other exalted persons. It was freezing hard and blowing too; yet not for a moment did we feel the cold. The snow blew in our faces, into our eyes and mouths, soaked through our puttees, got into our boots and dripped from our woollen caps. But we did not care. The collecting-box grew heavier, and the list of names in the book longer and more extravagant, each trying to outdo the other.

Mile after mile we went, fighting against the wind, falling into snowdrifts, and navigating by the lights of the houses. And yet we never saw our audience. We called at house after house; we sang in courtyards and porches, outside windows, or in the damp gloom of hallways; we heard voices from hidden rooms; we smelt rich clothes and strange hot food; we saw maids bearing in dishes or carrying away coffee cups; we received nuts, cakes, figs, preserved ginger, dates, cough-drops and money; but we never once saw our patrons. We sang as it were at the castle walls, and apart from the Squire, who had shown himself to prove that he was still alive, we never expected it otherwise.

As the night drew on there was trouble with Boney. 'Noël', for instance, had a rousing harmony which Boney persisted in singing, and singing flat. The others forbade him to sing it at all, and Boney said he would fight us. Picking himself up, he agreed we were right, then he disappeared altogether. He just turned away and walked into the snow and wouldn't answer when we called him back. Much later, as we reached a far point up the valley, somebody said 'Hark!' and we stopped to listen. Far away across the fields from the distant village came the sound of a frail voice singing, singing 'Noël', and singing it flat – it was Boney, branching out on his own.

We approached our last house high up on the hill, the place of Joseph the farmer. For him we had chosen a special carol, which was about the other Joseph, so that we always felt that singing it added a spicy cheek to the night. The last stretch of country to reach his farm was perhaps the most difficult of all. In these rough bare lanes, open to all winds, sheep were buried and wagons lost. Huddled together, we tramped in one another's footsteps, powdered snow blew into our screwed-up eyes, the candles burnt low, some blew out altogether, and we talked loudly above the gale.

Crossing, at last, the frozen mill-stream – whose wheel in summer still turned a barren mechanism – we climbed up to

Joseph's farm. Sheltered by trees, warm on its bed of snow, it seemed always to be like this. As always it was late; as always this was our final call. The snow had a fine crust upon it, and the old trees sparkled like tinsel.

We grouped ourselves round the farmhouse porch. The sky cleared, and broad streams of stars ran down over the valley and away to Wales. On Slad's white slopes, seen through the black sticks of its woods, some red lamps still burned in the windows.

Everything was quiet; everywhere there was the faint crackling silence of the winter night. We started singing, and we were all moved by the words and the sudden trueness of our voices. Pure, very clear, and breathless we sang:

> As Joseph was a walking
> He heard an angel sing;
> 'This night shall be the birth-time
> Of Christ the Heavenly King.
>
> He neither shall be bornèd
> In Housen nor in hall,
> Not in a place of paradise
> But in an ox's stall...

And 2,000 Christmases became real to us then; the houses, the halls, the places of paradise had all been visited; the stars were bright to guide the Kings through the snow; and across the farmyard we could hear the beasts in their stalls. We were given roast apples and hot mince-pies, in our nostrils were spices like myrrh, and in our wooden box, as we headed back for the village, there were golden gifts for all.

WILLIAM WORDSWORTH

from *The River Duddon*

The minstrels played their Christmas tune
To-night beneath my cottage eaves;
While, smitten by a lofty moon,
The encircling laurels, thick with leaves,
Gave back a rich and dazzling sheen,
That overpowered their natural green.

Through hill and valley every breeze
Had sunk to rest with folded wings:
Keen was the air, but could not freeze
Nor check the music of the strings;
So stout and hardy were the band
That scraped the chords with strenuous hand.

And who but listened? – till was paid
Respect to every inmate's claim;
The greeting given, the music played
In honour of each household name,
Duly pronounced with lusty call,
And 'Merry Christmas' wished to all!

Emily Brontë

from *Wuthering Heights*

AFTER PLAYING lady's-maid to the new comer, and putting my cakes in the oven, and making the house and kitchen cheerful with great fires, befitting Christmas eve, I prepared to sit down and amuse myself by singing carols, all alone; regardless of Joseph's affirmations that he considered the merry tunes I chose as next door to songs.

He had retired to private prayer in his chamber, and Mr and Mrs Earnshaw were engaging Missy's attention by sundry gay trifles bought for her to present to the little Lintons, as an acknowledgment of their kindness.

They had invited them to spend the morrow at Wuthering Heights, and the invitation had been accepted, on one condition: Mrs Linton begged that her darlings might be kept carefully apart from that 'naughty swearing boy'.

Under these circumstances I remained solitary. I smelt the rich scent of the heating spices; and admired the shining kitchen utensils, the polished clock, decked in holly, the silver mugs ranged on a tray ready to be filled with mulled ale for supper; and above all, the speckless purity of my particular care – the scoured and well-swept floor.

I gave due inward applause to every object and, then, I remembered how old Earnshaw used to come in when all was tidied, and call me a cant lass, and slip a shilling into my hand as a Christmas box; and, from that, I went on to think of his fondness for Heathcliff, and his dread lest he should suffer neglect after death had removed him; and that naturally led me to consider the poor lad's situation now, and from singing I changed my mind to crying. It struck me soon, however, there would be more sense in endeavouring to repair some of his wrongs than shedding tears over them – I got up and walked into the court to seek him.

He was not far; I found him smoothing the glossy coat of the new pony in the stable, and feeding the other beasts, according to custom.

'Make haste, Heathcliff!' I said, 'the kitchen is so comfortable – and Joseph is upstairs: make haste, and let me dress you smart before Miss Cathy comes out, and then you can sit together, with the whole hearth to yourselves, and have a long chatter till bedtime.'

He proceeded with his task and never turned his head towards me.

'Come – are you coming?' I continued. 'There's a little cake for each of you, nearly enough; and you'll need half an hour's donning.'

I waited five minutes, but getting no answer left him. Catherine supped with her brother and sister-in-law: Joseph and I joined at an unsociable meal, seasoned with reproofs on one side, and sauciness on the other. His cake and cheese remained on the table all night, for the fairies.

Charles Dickens

from *A Christmas Carol*

'Yo ho, my boys!' said Fezziwig. 'No more work to-night. Christmas Eve, Dick. Christmas, Ebenezer! Let's have the shutters up' cried old Fezziwig, with a sharp clap of his hands, 'before a man can say Jack Robinson!'

You wouldn't believe how those two fellows went at it! They charged into the street with the shutters – one, two, three – had 'em up in their places – four, five, six – barred 'em and pinned 'em – seven, eight, nine – and came back before you could have got to twelve, panting like race-horses.

'Hilli-ho!' cried old Fezziwig, skipping down from the high desk, with wonderful agility. 'Clear away, my lads, and let's have lots of room here! Hilli-ho, Dick! Chirrup, Ebenezer!'

Clear away! There was nothing they wouldn't have cleared away, or couldn't have cleared away, with old Fezziwig looking on. It was done in a minute. Every movable was packed off, as if it were dismissed from public life for evermore; the floor was swept and watered, the lamps were trimmed, fuel was heaped upon the fire; and the warehouse was as snug, and warm, and dry, and bright a ball-room, as you would desire to see upon a winter's night.

In came a fiddler with a music-book, and went up to the lofty desk, and made an orchestra of it, and tuned like fifty stomach-aches. In came Mrs Fezziwig, one vast substantial smile. In came the three Miss Fezziwigs, beaming and lovable. In came the six

young followers whose hearts they broke. In came all the young men and women employed in the business. In came the housemaid, with her cousin, the baker. In came the cook, with her brother's particular friend, the milkman. In came the boy from over the way, who was suspected of not having board enough from his master; trying to hide himself behind the girl from next door but one, who was proved to have had her ears pulled by her mistress. In they all came, one after another; some shyly, some boldly, some gracefully, some awkwardly, some pushing, some pulling; in they all came, anyhow and everyhow. Away they all went, twenty couple at once; hands half round and back again the other way; down the middle and up again; round and round in various stages of affectionate grouping; old top couple always turning up in the wrong place; new top couple starting off again, as soon as they got there; all top couples at last, and not a bottom one to help them! When this result was brought about, old Fezziwig, clapping his hands to stop the dance, cried out, 'Well done!' and the fiddler plunged his hot face into a pot of porter, especially provided for that purpose. But scorning rest, upon his reappearance, he instantly began again, though there were no dancers yet, as if the other fiddler had been carried home exhausted on a shutter, and he were a bran-new man resolved to beat him out of sight, or perish.

There were more dances, and there were forfeits, and more dances, and there was cake, and there was negus, and there was a great piece of Cold Roast, and there was a great piece of Cold Boiled, and there were mince-pies, and plenty of beer. But the great effect of the evening came after the Roast and Boiled, when the fiddler (an artful dog, mind! – the sort of man who knew his business better than you or I could have told it him!) struck up 'Sir Roger de Coverley'. Then old Fezziwig stood out to dance with Mrs Fezziwig. Top couple, too, with a good stiff piece of work cut out for them; three or four and twenty pair of partners; people who were not to be trifled with; people who *would* dance, and had no notion of walking.

But if they had been twice as many – ah, four times – old Fezziwig would have been a match for them, and so would Mrs Fezziwig. As to *her*, she was worthy to be his partner in every sense of the term. If that's not high praise, tell me higher, and I'll use it. A positive light appeared to issue from Fezziwig's calves. They shone in every part of the dance like moons. You couldn't have predicted, at any given time, what would have become of them next. And when old Fezziwig and Mrs Fezziwig had gone all through the dance; advance and retire, both hands to your partner, bow and curtsey, corkscrew, thread-the-needle, and back again to your place; Fezziwig 'cut' – cut so deftly, that he appeared to wink with his legs, and came upon his feet again without a stagger.

When the clock struck eleven, this domestic ball broke up. Mr and Mrs Fezziwig took their stations, one on either side of the door, and shaking hands with every person individually as he or she went out, wished him or her a Merry Christmas.

Thomas Hardy

The Oxen

Christmas Eve, and twelve of the clock.
   'Now they are all on their knees,'
An elder said as we sat in a flock
   By the embers in hearthside ease.

We pictured the meek mild creatures where
   They dwelt in their strawy pen,
Nor did it occur to one of us there
   To doubt they were kneeling then.

So fair a fancy few would weave
   In these years! Yet, I feel,
If someone said on Christmas Eve,
   'Come; see the oxen kneel

'In the lonely barton by yonder coomb
   Our childhood used to know,'
I should go with him in the gloom,
   Hoping it might be so.

SAKI

Bertie's Christmas Eve

IT WAS Christmas Eve, and the family circle of Luke Steffink, Esq, was aglow with the amiability and random mirth which the occasion demanded. A long and lavish dinner had been partaken of, waits had been round and sung carols, the house-party had regaled itself with more carolling on its own account, and there had been romping which, even in a pulpit reference, could not have been condemned as ragging. In the midst of the general glow, however, there was one black unkindled cinder.

Bertie Steffink, nephew of the aforementioned Luke, had early in life adopted the profession of ne'er-do-weel; his father had been something of the kind before him. At the age of eighteen Bertie had commenced that round of visits to our Colonial possessions, so seemly and desirable in the case of a Prince of the Blood, so suggestive of insincerity in a young man of the middle-class. He had gone to grow tea in Ceylon and fruit in British Columbia, and to help sheep to grow wool in Australia. At the age of twenty he had just returned from some similar errand in Canada, from which it may be gathered that the trial he gave to these various experiments was of the summary drum-head nature. Luke Steffink, who fulfilled the troubled rôle of guardian and deputy-parent to Bertie, deplored the persistent manifestation of the homing instinct on his nephew's part, and his solemn thanks earlier in the day for the blessing of reporting a united family had no reference to Bertie's return.

Arrangements had been promptly made for packing the youth off to a distant corner of Rhodesia, whence return would be a difficult matter; the journey to this uninviting destination was imminent, in fact a more careful and willing traveller would have already begun to think about his packing. Hence Bertie was in no mood to share in the festive spirit which displayed itself around him, and resentment smouldered within him at the eager, self-absorbed discussion of social plans for the coming months which he heard on all sides. Beyond depressing his uncle and the family circle generally by singing 'Say au revoir, and not good-bye', he had taken no part in the evening's conviviality.

Eleven o'clock had struck some half-hour ago, and the elder Steffinks began to throw out suggestions leading up to that process which they called retiring for the night.

'Come, Teddie, it's time you were in your little bed, you know,' said Luke Steffink to his thirteen-year-old son.

'That's where we all ought to be,' said Mrs Steffink.

'There wouldn't be room,' said Bertie.

The remark was considered to border on the scandalous; everybody ate raisins and almonds with the nervous industry of sheep feeding during threatening weather.

'In Russia,' said Horace Bordenby, who was staying in the house as a Christmas guest, 'I've read that the peasants believe that if you go into a cow-house or stable at midnight on Christmas Eve you will hear the animals talk. They're supposed to have the gift of speech at that one moment of the year.'

'Oh, *do* let's *all* go down to the cow-house and listen to what they've got to say?' exclaimed Beryl, to whom anything was thrilling and amusing if you did it in a troop.

Mrs Steffink made a laughing protest, but gave a virtual consent by saying, 'We must all wrap up well, then'. The idea seemed a scatterbrained one to her, and almost heathenish, but it afforded an opportunity for 'throwing the young people together', and as such she welcomed it. Mr Horace Bordenby was a young man with quite substantial prospects, and he had danced with Beryl at a local subscription ball a sufficient number of times to warrant the authorised inquiry on the part of the neighbours whether 'there was anything in it'. Though Mrs Steffink would not have put it in so many words, she shared the idea of the Russian peasantry that on this night the beast might speak.

The cow-house stood at the junction of the garden with a small paddock, an isolated survival, in a suburban neighbourhood, of what had once been a small farm. Luke Steffink was complacently proud of his cow-house and his two cows; he felt that they gave him a stamp of solidity which no number of Wyandottes or Orpingtons could impart. They even seemed to link him in a sort of inconsequent way with those patriarchs who derived importance from their floating capital of flocks and herbs, he-asses and she-asses. It had been an anxious and momentous occasion when he had had to decide definitely between 'the Byre' and 'the Ranch' for the naming of his villa residence. A December midnight was hardly the moment he would have chosen for showing his farm-building to visitors, but since it was a fine night, and the young people were anxious for an excuse for a mild frolic, Luke consented to chaperon the expedition. The servants had long since gone to bed, so the house was left in the charge of Bertie, who scornfully declined to stir out on the pretext of listening to bovine conversation.

'We must go quietly,' said Luke, as he headed the procession of giggling young folk, brought up in the rear by the shawled and hooded figure of Mrs Steffink; 'I've always laid stress on keeping this a quiet and orderly neighbourhood.'

It was a few minutes to midnight when the party reached the cow-house and made its way in by the light of Luke's stable lantern. For a moment every one stood in silence, almost with a feeling of being in church.

'Daisy – the one lying down – is by a shorthorn bull out of a Guernsey cow,' announced Luke in a hushed voice, which was in keeping with the foregoing impression.

'Is she?' said Bordenby, rather as if he had expected her to be by Rembrandt.

'Myrtle is—'

Myrtle's family history was cut short by a little scream from the women of the party.

The cow-house door had closed noiselessly behind them and the key had turned gratingly in the lock; then they heard Bertie's voice pleasantly wishing them good-night and his footsteps retreating along the garden path.

Luke Steffink strode to the window; it was a small square opening of the old-fashioned sort, with iron bars let into the stonework.

'Unlock the door this instant,' he shouted, with as much air of menacing authority as a hen might assume when screaming through the bars of a coop at a marauding hawk. In reply to his summons the hall-door closed with a defiant bang.

A neighbouring clock struck the hour of midnight. If the cows had received the gift of human speech at that moment they would not have been able to make themselves heard. Seven or eight other voices were engaged in describing Bertie's present conduct and his general character at a high pressure of excitement and indignation.

In the course of half an hour or so everything that it was permissible to say about Bertie had been said some dozens of times, and other topics began to come to the front – the extreme mustiness of the cow-house, the possibility of it catching fire, and the probability of it being a Rowton House for the vagrant rats of the neighbourhood. And still no sign of deliverance came to the unwilling vigil-keepers.

Towards one o'clock the sound of rather boisterous and undisciplined carol-singing approached rapidly, and came to a sudden anchorage, apparently just outside the garden-gate. A motor-load of youthful 'bloods', in a high state of conviviality, had made a temporary halt for repairs; the stoppage, however, did not extend to the vocal efforts of the party, and the watchers in the cow-shed were treated to a highly unauthorised rendering of 'Good King Wenceslas', in which the adjective 'good' appeared to be very carelessly applied.

The noise had the effect of bringing Bertie out into the garden, but he utterly ignored the pale, angry faces peering out at the cow-house window, and concentrated his attention on the revellers outside the gate.

'Wassail, you chaps!' he shouted.

'Wassail, old sport!' they shouted back; 'we'd jolly well drink y'r health, only we've nothing to drink it in.'

'Come and wassail inside,' said Bertie hospitably; 'I'm all alone, and there's heaps of "wet".'

They were total strangers, but his touch of kindness made them instantly his kin. In another moment the unauthorised version of King Wenceslas, which, like many other scandals, grew worse on repetition, went echoing up the garden path; two of the revellers gave an impromptu performance on the way by executing the

31

staircase waltz up the terraces of what Luke Steffink, hitherto with some justification, called his rock-garden. The rock part of it was still there when the waltz had been accorded its third encore. Luke, more than ever like a cooped hen behind the cow-house bars, was in a position to realise the feelings of concert-goers unable to countermand the call for an encore which they neither desire or deserve.

The hall door closed with a bang on Bertie's guests, and the sounds of merriment became faint and muffled to the weary watchers at the other end of the garden. Presently two ominous pops, in quick succession, made themselves distinctly heard.

'They've got at the champagne!' exclaimed Mrs Steffink.

'Perhaps it's the sparkling Moselle,' said Luke hopefully.

Three or four more pops were heard.

'The champagne *and* the sparkling Moselle,' said Mrs Steffink.

Luke uncorked an expletive which, like brandy in a temperance household, was only used on rare emergencies. Mr Horace Bordenby had been making use of similar expressions under his breath for a considerable time past. The experiment of 'throwing the young people together' had been prolonged beyond a point when it was likely to produce any romantic result.

Some forty minutes later the hall door opened and disgorged a crowd that had thrown off any restraint of shyness that might have influenced its earlier actions. Its vocal efforts in the direction of carol singing were now supplemented by instrumental music; a Christmas-tree that had been prepared for the children of the gardener and other household retainers had yielded a rich spoil of tin trumpets, rattles, and drums. The life-story of King Wenceslas had been dropped, Luke was thankful to notice, but it was intensely irritating for the chilled prisoners in the cow-house to be told that it was 'a hot time in the old town tonight', together with some accurate but entirely superfluous information as to the imminence of Christmas morning. Judging by the protests which began to be shouted from the upper windows of neighbouring houses, the sentiments prevailing in the cow-house were heartily echoed in other quarters.

The revellers found their car, and, what was more remarkable, managed to drive off in it, with a parting fanfare of tin trumpets. The lively beat of a drum disclosed the fact that the master of the revels remained on the scene.

'Bertie!' came in an angry, imploring chorus of shouts and screams from the cow-house window.

'Hullo,' cried the owner of the name, turning his rather errant steps in the direction of the summons; 'are you people still there? Must have heard everything cows got to say by this time. If you haven't, no use waiting. After all, it's a Russian legend, and Russian Chrismush Eve not due for 'nother fortnight. Better come out.'

After one or two ineffectual attempts he managed to pitch the key of the cow-house door in through the window. Then, lifting his voice in the strains of 'I'm afraid to go home in the dark', with a lusty drum accompaniment, he led the way back to the house. The hurried procession of the released that followed in his steps came in for a good deal of the adverse comment that his exuberant display had evoked.

It was the happiest Christmas Eve he had ever spent. To quote his own words, he had a rotten Christmas.

AUBREY BEARDSLEY

THE NATIVITY

Christina Rossetti

A Christmas Carol

In the bleak mid-winter
  Frosty wind made moan,
Earth stood hard as iron,
  Water like a stone;
Snow had fallen, snow on snow,
  Snow on snow,
In the bleak mid-winter
  Long ago.

Our God, Heaven cannot hold Him
  Nor earth sustain;
Heaven and earth shall flee away
  When He comes to reign:
In the bleak mid-winter
  A stable-place sufficed
The Lord God Almighty
  Jesus Christ.

Enough for Him whom cherubim
  Worship night and day,
A breastful of milk
  And a mangerful of hay;
Enough for Him, whom angels
  Fall down before,
The ox and ass and camel
  Which adore.

Angels and archangels
   May have gathered there,
Cherubim and seraphim
   Thronged the air;
But only His mother
   In her maiden bliss
Worshipped the Beloved
   With a kiss.

What can I give Him,
   Poor as I am?
If I were a shepherd
   I would bring a lamb,
If I were a Wise Man
   I would do my part, –
Yet what I can I give Him,
   Give my heart.

JOHN MILTON

from *On the Morning of Christ's Nativity*

I

This is the month, and this the happy morn
Wherein the Son of Heav'n's eternal King,
Of wedded Maid, and Virgin Mother born,
Our great redemption from above did bring;
For so the holy sages once did sing,
    That he our deadly forfeit should release,
And with his Father work us a perpetual peace.

II

That glorious Form, that Light unsufferable,
And that far-beaming blaze of Majesty,
Wherewith he wont at Heav'n's high Council-Table,
To sit the midst of Trinal Unity,
He laid aside; and here with us to be,
    Forsook the Courts of everlasting Day,
And chose with us a darksome House of mortal Clay.

III

Say Heav'nly Muse, shall not thy sacred vein
Afford a present to the Infant God?
Hast thou no verse, no hymn, or solemn strain,
To welcome him to this his new abode,
Now while the Heav'n, by the Sun's team untrod,
    Hath took no print of the approaching light,
And all the spangled host keep watch in squadrons bright?

'OEVS IXOIVTORIV MEV ITEIT OE OTTE ROIVO

IV

See how from far upon the Eastern road
The star-led Wizards haste with odours sweet,
O run, prevent them with thy humble ode,
And lay it lowly at his blessed feet;
Have thou the honour first, thy Lord to greet,
    And join thy voice unto the Angel Quire,
From out his secret Altar toucht with hallow'd fire.

Elizabeth Barrett Browning

from *The Virgin Mary to the Child Jesus*

We sate among the stalls at Bethlehem.
The dumb kine from their fodder turning them,
   Softened their hornèd faces,
   To almost human gazes
   Toward the newly Born.
The simple shepherds from the star-lit brooks
   Brought visionary looks,
As yet in their astonied hearing rung
   The strange sweet angel-tongue.
The maji of the East, in sandals worn,
   Knelt reverent, sweeping round,
With long, pale beards, their gifts upon the ground,
   The incense, myrrh, and gold
These baby hands were impotent to hold.
So, let all earthlies and celestials wait
   Upon thy royal state.
   Sleep, sleep, my kingly One!

G.K. CHESTERTON

A Christmas Carol

The Christ-child lay on Mary's lap,
  His hair was like a light.
(O weary, weary were the world,
  But here is all aright.)

The Christ-child lay on Mary's breast
  His hair was like a star.
(O stern and cunning are the kings,
  But here the true hearts are.)

The Christ-child lay on Mary's heart,
  His hair was like a fire.
(O weary, weary is the world,
  But here the world's desire.)

The Christ-child stood on Mary's knee,
  His hair was like a crown,
And all the flowers looked up at Him,
  And all the stars looked down.

John Donne

Nativity

Immensity, cloister'd in thy dear womb,
Now leaves His well-belov'd imprisonment,
There he hath made himself to his intent
Weak enough, now, into our world to come.
But O!, for thee, for Him, hath th'inn no room?
Yet lay Him in this stall, and from th'Orient,
Stars and wise men will travel to prevent
The effects of Herod's jealous general doom.
See'st thou, my soul, with thy faith's eye, how He
Which fills all place, yet none holds Him, doth lie?
Was not His pity towards thee wondrous high,
That would have need to be pitied by thee?
Kiss Him, and with Him into Egypt go
With his kind mother, who partakes thy woe.

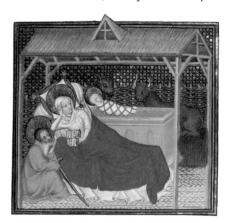

CHRISTMAS DAY

SAMUEL PEPYS

from his *Diary*

25 DECEMBER 1662

CHRISTMAS DAY. Had a pleasant walk to White Hall, where I intended to have received the Communion with the family, but I came a little too late. So I walked up into the house and spent my time looking over pictures, particularly the ships in King Henry the VIIIth's Voyage to Bullaen [Boulogne]; marking the great difference between those built then and now. By and by down to the chapel again, where Bishop Morley preached upon the song of the Angels, 'Glory to God on high, on earth peace, and good will towards men'. Methought he made but a poor sermon, but long, and, reprehending the common jollity of the Court for the true joy that shall and ought to be on these days, he particularized concerning their excess in playes and gaming, saying that he whose office it is to keep the gamesters in order and within bounds serves but for a second rather in a duell, meaning the groome-porter. Upon which it was worth observing how far they are come from taking the reprehensions of a bishop seriously, that they all laugh in the chapel when he reflected on their ill actions and courses. He did much press us to joy in these public days of joy, and to hospitality; but one that stood by whispered in my eare that the Bishop himself do not spend one groate to the poor. The sermon done, a good anthem followed, with vialls, and the King came down to receive the Sacrament. But I staid not, but calling

my boy from my Lord's lodgings, and giving Sarah some good advice by my Lord's order to be sober, and look after the house, I walked home again with great pleasure, and there dined by my wife's bedside with great content, having a mess of brave plum-porridge and a roasted pullet for dinner, and I sent for a mince-pie abroad, my wife not being well, to make any herself yet.

ANNE BRONTË

Music on Christmas Morning

Music I love – but never strain
   Could kindle raptures so divine,
So grief assuage, so conquer pain,
   And rouse this pensive heart of mine –
As that we hear on Christmas morn,
Upon the wintry breezes borne.

Though Darkness still her empire keep,
   And hours must pass, ere morning break;
From troubled dreams, or slumbers deep,
   That music *kindly* bids us wake:
It calls us, with an angel's voice,
To wake, and worship, and rejoice;

To greet with joy the glorious morn,
   Which angels welcomed long ago,
When our redeeming Lord was born,
   To bring the light of Heaven below;
The Powers of Darkness to dispel,
And rescue Earth from Death and Hell.

While listening to that sacred strain,
   My raptured spirit soars on high;
I seem to hear those songs again
   Resounding through the open sky,
That kindled such divine delight,
In those who watched their flocks by night.

With them I celebrate His birth –
  Glory to God in highest Heaven,
Good-will to men, and peace on earth,
  To us a Saviour-king is given;
Our God is come to claim His own,
And Satan's power is overthrown!

A sinless God, for sinful men,
  Descends to suffer and to bleed;
Hell *must* renounce its empire then;
  The price is paid, the world is freed,
And Satan's self must now confess,
That Christ has earned a *Right* to bless:

Now holy Peace may smile from Heaven,
  And heavenly Truth from earth shall spring:
The captive's galling bonds are riven,
  For our Redeemer is our King;
And He that gave His blood for men
Will lead us home to God again.

from *Orley Farm*

IT WAS a mile to the church, and Miss Furnival knew the advantage of appearing in her seat unfatigued and without subjection to wind, mud, or rain. 'I must confess,' she said, 'that under all the circumstances, I shall prefer your mother's company to yours;' whereupon Staveley, in the completion of his arrangements, assigned the other places in the carriage to the married ladies of the company.

'But I have taken your sister Madeline's seat in the carriage,' protested Sophia with great dismay.

'My sister Madeline generally walks.'

'Then of course I shall walk with her;' but when the time came Miss Furnival did go in the carriage whereas Miss Staveley went on foot.

It so fell out, as they started, that Graham found himself walking at Miss Staveley's side, to the great disgust, no doubt, of half a dozen other aspirants for that honour. 'I cannot help thinking,' he said, as they stepped briskly over the crisp white frost, 'that this Christmas-day of ours is a great mistake.'

'Oh, Mr Graham!' she exclaimed

'You need not regard me with horror, – at least not with any special horror on this occasion.'

'But what you say is very horrid.'

'That, I flatter myself, seems so only because I have not yet said it. That part of our Christmas-day which is made to be in any degree sacred is by no means a mistake.'

'I am glad you think that.'

'Or rather, it is not a mistake in as far as it is in any degree made sacred. But the peculiar conviviality of the day is so ponderous! Its roast-beefiness oppresses one so thoroughly from the first moment of one's waking, to the last ineffectual effort at a bit of fried pudding for supper!'

'But you need not eat fried pudding for supper. Indeed, here, I am afraid, you will not have any supper offered you at all.'

'No; not to me individually, under that name. I might also manage to guard my own self under any such offers. But there is always the flavour of the sweetmeat, in the air, – of all the sweetmeats edible and non-edible.'

'You begrudge the children their snap-dragon. That's what it all means, Mr Graham.'

'No; I deny it; unpremeditated snap-dragon is dear to my soul; and I could expend myself in blindman's buff.'

'You shall then, after dinner; for of course you know that we all dine early.'

'But blindman's buff at three, with snap-dragon at a quarter to four – charades at five, with wine and sweet cake at half-past six, is ponderous. And that's our mistake. The big turkey would be very good; – capital fun to see a turkey twice as big as it ought to be! But the big turkey, and the mountain of beef, and the pudding weighing a hundredweight, oppress one's spirits by their combined gravity. And then they impart a memory of indigestion, a halo as it were of apoplexy, even to the church services.'

'I do not agree with you the least in the world.'

'I ask you to answer me fairly. Is not additional eating an ordinary Englishman's ordinary idea of Christmas-day?'

49

'I am only an ordinary Englishwoman and therefore cannot say. It is not my idea.'

'I believe that the ceremony, as kept by us, is perpetuated by the butchers and beersellers, with a helping hand from the grocers. It is essentially a material festival; and I would not object to it even on that account if it were not so grievously overdone. How the sun is moistening the frost on the ground. As we come back the road will be quite wet.'

'We shall be going home then and it will not signify. Remember, Mr Graham, I shall expect you to come forward in great strength for blindman's buff.' As he gave her the required promise, he thought that even the sports of Christmas-day would be bearable, if she also were to make one of the sportsmen; and then they entered the church.

I do not know of anything more pleasant to the eye than a pretty country church, decorated for Christmas-day. The effect in a city is altogether different. I will not say that churches there should not be decorated, but comparatively it is a matter of indifference. No one knows who does it. The peculiar munificence of the squire who has sacrificed his holly bushes is not appreciated. The work of the fingers that have been employed is not recognised. The efforts made for hanging the pendent wreaths to each capital have been of no special interest to any large number of the worshippers. It has been done by contract, probably, and even if well done has none of the grace of association. But here at Noningsby church, the winter flowers had been cut by Madeline and the gardener, and the red berries had been grouped by her own hands. She and the vicar's wife had stood together with perilous audacity on the top of the clerk's desk while they fixed the branches beneath the cushion of the old-fashioned turret, from which the sermons were preached. And all this had of course been talked about at the house; and some of the party had gone over to see, including Sophia Furnival, who had declared that nothing could be so delightful, though she had omitted to endanger her fingers by any participation in the work. And the children had regarded the operation as a triumph of all that was wonderful in decoration; and thus many of them had been made happy.

ROBERT LOUIS STEVENSON

Christmas at Sea

The sheets were frozen hard, and they cut the naked hand;
The decks were like a slide, where a seaman scarce could stand;
The wind was a nor'-wester, blowing squally off the sea;
And cliffs and spouting breakers were the only things a-lee.

They heard the surf a-roaring before the break of day;
But 'twas only with the peep of light we saw how ill we lay.
We tumbled every hand on deck instanter, with a shout,
And we gave her the maintops'l, and stood by to go about.

All day we tacked and tacked between the South Head and the
    North;
All day we hauled the frozen sheets, and got no further forth;
All day as cold as charity, in bitter pain and dread,
For very life and nature we tacked from head to head.

We gave the South a wider berth, for there the tide-race roared;
But every tack we made we brought the North Head close aboard.
So's we saw the cliff and houses, and the breakers running high,
And the coastguard in his garden, with his glass against his eye.

The frost was on the village roofs as white as ocean foam;
The good red fires were burning bright in every 'longshore home;
The windows sparkled clear, and the chimneys volleyed out;
And I vow we sniffed the victuals as the vessel went about.

The bells upon the church were rung with a mighty jovial cheer;
For it's just that I should tell you how (of all days in the year)
This day of our adversity was blessèd Christmas morn,
And the house above the coastguard's was the house where I
    was born.

O well I saw the pleasant room, the pleasant faces there,
My mother's silver spectacles, my father's silver hair;
And well I saw the firelight, like a flight of homely elves,
Go dancing round the china plates that stand upon the shelves.

And well I knew the talk they had, the talk that was of me,
Of the shadow on the household and the son that went to sea;
And O the wicked fool I seemed, in every kind of way,
To be here and hauling frozen ropes on blessèd Christmas Day.

They lit the high sea-light, and the dark began to fall.
'All hands to loose topgallant sails,' I heard the captain call.
'By the Lord, she'll never stand it,' our first mate, Jackson, cried.
… 'It's the one way or the other, Mr Jackson,' he replied.

She staggered to her bearings, but the sails were new and good,
And the ship smelt up to windward just as though
    she understood.
As the winter's day was ending, in the entry of the night,
We cleared the weary headland, and passed below the light.

And they heaved a mighty breath, every soul on board but me,
As they saw her nose again pointing handsome out to sea;
But all that I could think of, in the darkness and the cold,
Was just that I was leaving home and my folks were growing old.

George Eliot

from *The Mill on the Floss*

FINE OLD CHRISTMAS, with the snowy hair and ruddy face, had done his duty that year in the noblest fashion, and had set off his rich gifts of warmth and colour with all the heightening contrast of frost and snow.

Snow lay on the croft and river-bank in undulations softer than the limbs of infancy; it lay with the neatliest finished border on every sloping roof, making the dark-red gables stand out with a new depth of colour; it weighed heavily on the laurels and fir-trees, till it fell from them with a shuddering sound; it clothed the rough turnip-field with whiteness, and made the sheep look like dark blotches; the gates were all blocked up with the sloping drifts, and here and there a disregarded four-footed beast stood as if petrified 'in unrecumbent sadness'; there was no gleam, no shadow, for the heavens, too, were one still, pale cloud – no sound or motion in any thing but the dark river, that flowed and moaned like an unresting sorrow. But old Christmas smiled as he laid this cruel-seeming spell on the out-door world, for he meant to light up home with new brightness, to deepen all the richness of in-door colour, and give a keener edge of delight to the warm fragrance of food: he meant to prepare a sweet imprisonment that would strengthen the primitive fellowship of kindred, and make the sunshine of familiar human faces as welcome as the hidden day-star. His kindness fell but hardly on the homeless – fell but hardly on the homes where the hearth was not very warm, and where the food had little fragrance; where the human faces had no sunshine in them, but rather the leaden, blank-eyed gaze of unexpectant want. But the fine old season meant well; and if he has not learned the secret how to bless men impartially, it is because his father Time, with ever-unrelenting purpose, still hides that secret in his own mighty, slow-beating heart.

And yet this Christmas day, in spite of Tom's fresh delight in home, was not, he thought, somehow or other, quite so happy as it had always been before. The red berries were just as abundant on the holly, and he and Maggie had dressed all the windows, and mantlepieces, and picture-frames on Christmas eve with as much taste as ever, wedding the thick-set scarlet clusters with branches of the black-berried ivy. There had been singing under the windows after midnight – supernatural singing, Maggie always felt, in spite of Tom's contemptuous insistence that the singers were old Patch, the parish clerk, and the rest of the church choir: she trembled with awe when their carolling broke in upon her dreams, and the image of men in fustian clothes was always thrust away by the vision of angels resting on the parted cloud. But the midnight chant had helped as usual to lift the morning above the level of common days; and then there was the smell of hot toast and ale from the kitchen, at the breakfast hour; the favourite anthem, the green boughs, and the short sermon gave the appropriate festal character to the church-going; and aunt and uncle Moss, with all their eight children, were looking like so many reflectors of the bright parlour-fire, when the church-goers came back, stamping the snow from their feet. The plum-pudding was of the same handsome roundness as ever, and came in with the symbolic blue flames around it, as if it had been heroically snatched from the nether fires into which it had been thrown by dyspeptic Puritans;

the dessert was as splendid as ever, with its golden oranges, brown nuts, and the crystalline light and dark of apple jelly and damson cheese: in all these things Christmas was as it had always been since Tom could remember; it was only distinguished, if by anything, by superior sliding and snowballs.

Rudyard Kipling

Christmas in India

Dim dawn behind the tamarisks – the sky is saffron-yellow –
As the women in the village grind the corn,
And the parrots seek the river-side, each calling to his fellow
That the Day, the staring Eastern Day is born.
Oh, the white dust on the highway! Oh, the stenches in the
    byway!
Oh, the clammy fog that hovers o'er the earth!
And at Home they're making merry 'neath the white and scarlet
    berry –
What part have India's exiles in their mirth?

Full day behind the tamarisks – the sky is blue and staring –
As the cattle crawl afield beneath the yoke,
And they bear One o'er the field-path, who is past all hope or
    caring,
To the ghat below the curling wreaths of smoke.
Call on Rama, going slowly, as ye bear a brother lowly –
Call on Rama – he may hear, perhaps, your voice!
With our hymn-books and our psalters we appeal to other
    altars,
And today we bid 'good Christian men rejoice!'

High noon behind the tamarisks – the sun is hot above us –
As at Home the Christmas Day is breaking wan.
They will drink our healths at dinner – those who tell us how
    they love us,

And forget us till another year be gone!
Oh, the toil that knows no breaking! Oh the *Heimweh*,
    ceaseless, aching!
Oh, the black dividing Sea and alien Plain!
Youth was cheap – wherefore we sold it. Gold was good
    – we hoped to hold it,
And today we know the fulness of our gain.

Grey dusk behind the tamarisks – the parrots fly together –
As the sun is sinking slowly over Home;
And his last ray seems to mock us shackled in a lifelong tether
That drags us back howe'er so far we roam.
Hard her service, poor her payment – she in ancient, tattered
    raiment –
India, she the grim Stepmother of our kind.
If a year of life be lent her, if her temple's shrine we enter,
The door is shut – we may not look behind.

Black night behind the tamarisks – the owls begin their chorus –
As the conches from the temple scream and bray.
With the fruitless years behind us, and the hopeless years before
    us,
Let us honour, Oh, my brothers, Christmas Day!
Call a truce, then, to our labours – let us feast with friends and
    neighbours,
And be merry as the custom of our caste;
For if 'faint and forced the laughter,' and if sadness follow after,
We are richer by one mocking Christmas past.

Thomas Haynes Bayly

The Mistletoe Bough

The mistletoe hung in the castle hall,
The holly branch shone on the old oak wall;
And the baron's retainers were blithe and gay,
And keeping the Christmas holiday.
The baron beheld, with a father's pride;
His beautiful child, young Lovell's bride;
While she, with her bright eyes, seem'd to be
The star of that goodly company.

'I'm weary of dancing, now,' she cried;
'Here tarry a moment – I'll hide – I'll hide!
And, Lovell, be sure thou'rt first to trace
The clue to my secret hiding place.'
Away she ran – and her friends began
Each tower to search, and each nook to scan;
And young Lovell cried, 'Oh! where do you hide?
I'm lonesome without thee, my own fair bride.'

They sought her that night! and they sought her next day!
And they sought her in vain, when a week pass'd away!
In the highest – the lowest – the loneliest spot,
Young Lovell sought wildly – but found her not.
And years flew by, and their brief at last
Was told as a sorrowful tale long past;
And when Lovell appear'd the children cried,
'See! the old man weeps for his fairy bride.'

At length, an old chest, that had long laid hid
Was found in the castle – they raised the lid –
And a skeleton form lay mouldering there,
In the bridal wreath of that lady fair!
Oh! sad was her fate! – in sportive jest
She hid from her lord in the old oak chest.
It closed with a spring! – and a dreadful doom,
The bride lay clasp'd in her living tomb!

NANCY MITFORD

from *Christmas Pudding*

CHRISTMAS DAY itself was organized by Lady Bobbin with the thoroughness and attention to detail of a general leading his army into battle. Not one moment of its enjoyment was left to chance or to the ingenuity of her guests; these received on Christmas Eve their marching orders, orders which must be obeyed to the letter on pain of death. Even Lady Bobbin, however, superwoman though she might be, could not prevent the day from being marked by a good deal of crossness, much over-eating, and a series of startling incidents.

The battle opened, as it were, with the Christmas stockings. These, in thickest worsted, bought specially for the occasion, were handed to the guests just before bedtime on Christmas Eve, with instructions that they were to be hung up on their bedposts by means of huge safety pins, which were also distributed. Lady Bobbin and her confederate, Lord Leamington Spa, then allowed a certain time to elapse until, judging that Morpheus would have descended upon the household, they sallied forth together (he arrayed in a white wig, beard and eyebrows and red dressing-gown, she clasping a large basket full of suitable presents) upon a stealthy noctambulation, during the course of which every stocking was neatly filled. The objects thus distributed were exactly the same every year, a curious and wonderful assort-ment including a pocket handkerchief, Old Moore's Almanack, a balloon not as yet blown up, a mouth organ, a ball of string, a penknife, an instrument for taking stones out of horses' shoes, a book of jokes, a puzzle, and, deep down in the woolly toe of the stocking, whence it would emerge in a rather hairy condition, a chocolate baby. Alas! Most of Lady Bobbin's guests felt that they would willingly have forgone these delightful but inexpensive objects in return for the night's sleep of which they were thus deprived. Forewarned though they were, the shadowy and terrifying appearance of Lord Leamington Spa fumbling about the foot of their beds in the light of a flickering candle gave most of them such a fearful start that all thoughts of sleep were banished for many hours to come.

For the lucky ones who did manage to doze off a rude shock was presently in store. At about five o'clock in the morning Master Christopher Robin Chadlington made a tour of the bedrooms, and having awoken each occupant in turn with a blast of his mouth organ, announced in a voice fraught with tragedy that Auntie Gloria had forgotten to put a chocolate baby in his stocking. 'Please might I have a bit of yours?' This quaint ruse was only too successful, and Christopher Robin acquired thereby no fewer than fourteen chocolate babies, all of which he ate before breakfast. The consequences, which were appalling, took place under the dining-room table at a moment when everybody else was busily opening the Christmas post. After this, weak but cheerful, young Master Chadlington spent the rest of the day in bed practising on his mouth organ.

By luncheon time any feelings of Christmas goodwill which the day and the religious service, duly attended by all, might have been expected to produce had quite evaporated, and towards the end of that meal the dining-room echoed with sounds of furious argument among the grown-ups. It was the duchess who began it.

She said, in a clear, ringing voice which she knew must penetrate to the consciousness of Lady Bobbin:

'Yes, the day of the capitalist is over now; and a jolly good thing too.'

'May I ask,' said Lady Bobbin, rising like a trout to this remark and leaning across the projecting stomach of Lord Leamington Spa, 'why you, of all people, think that a good thing? Mind you, I don't admit that the capitalist system has come to an end, of course it hasn't, but why should you pretend to be pleased if it did? Affectation, I should call it.'

'No, not entirely affectation, Gloria darling. What I mean is that if, in a few years' time, people like us have no money left for luxuries we shall all, as a consequence, lead simpler and better lives. More fresh air, more sleep, more time to think and read. No night clubs, no Ritz, no Blue Train, less rushing about. And the result of that will be that we shall all be much happier. Don't you agree?'

Lady Bobbin, whose life was quite innocent of night clubs, the Ritz, and the Blue Train, and who had more time than she wanted in which to think and read, was not impressed by this statement. 'It has never been necessary to make a fool of oneself just because one happens to have money. There have always been plenty of decent people in the world, but unfortunately nobody ever hears about them, because they don't advertise themselves like the others. I wonder, Louisa, whether you will be quite so glad of the end of capitalism when you find yourself without the common necessities of life.'

'I don't anticipate that,' said the duchess comfortably. 'The world at present is suffering from over-production, not under-production, of the necessities of life.'

'Surely, duchess,' began Captain Chadlington ponderously, from his end of the table, feeling that now, if ever, was the time to make use of the information that he had so laboriously garnered from the P.M., the F.O., the I.L.P., S.B., L.G., and his fellow M.P.s, and to assert himself as a rising young politician. The duchess, however, took no notice of him and continued to goad Lady Bobbin.

'Think,' she said, 'how splendid it will be for our characters as a class if we are forced to lead simple, healthy lives, to look after our own children, and to earn our own bread. And then think of all the horrors that will be done away with, all those ghastly hideous country houses everywhere that will be pulled down. We shall be able to live in darling clean little cottages instead –'

'My house,' said Lady Bobbin, always quick to take offence, 'is, I hope, scrupulously kept. If you are implying—'

'Darling, don't be absurd. I only meant that they would be spiritually clean.'

'If you feel like this, Louisa,' said Lord Leamington Spa, now entering the lists with the light of battle in his eye, 'why on earth don't you act accordingly? Why not shut up Brackenhampton and live in one of the cottages there instead? I don't suppose there's anything to prevent you.'

'Nothing to prevent me, indeed!' cried the duchess. She had been waiting for this argument to be produced like a cat waiting for a mouse. 'There are nearly a hundred living souls to prevent me, that's all. D'you realize that we employ altogether ninety-eight people in the house and gardens at Brackenhampton? I can't, for no reason at all, take a step which would deprive all those old friends of work, food, even of a shelter over their heads. It would be quite unthinkable. I only say that if the whole system by which we live at present were to be changed we ourselves would all be a good deal happier than we are, and better in every way.'

Lady Bobbin said 'Pooh!' and rose to leave the table. She was trembling with fury.

The afternoon was so wet and foggy, so extremely unseasonable, in fact, that Lady Bobbin was obliged with the utmost reluctance to abandon the paper chase which she had organized. Until four o'clock, therefore, the house party was left to enjoy in peace that exquisite discomfort which can only be produced by overfed slumberings in arm-chairs. At four punctually everybody assembled in the ballroom while for nearly an hour the Woodford schoolchildren mummed. It was the Woodford schoolchildren's annual burden to mum at Christmas; it was the annual burden of the inhabitants of Compton Bobbin to watch the mumming. Both sides, however, bore this infliction with fortitude, and no further awkwardness took place until after tea, when Lord Leamington Spa, having donned once more his dressing-gown and wig, was distributing gifts from the laden branches of the Christmas Tree. This was the big moment of the day. The tree, of course, immediately caught fire, but this was quite a usual occurrence, and the butler had no difficulty in putting it out. The real crisis occurred when Lady Bobbin opened the largish, square parcel which had 'To darling Mummy from her very loving little Bobby' written on it, and which to Lady Bobbin's rage and horror was found to contain a volume entitled *The Sexual Life of Savages in Northern Melanesia*. This classic had been purchased at great expense by poor Bobby as a present for Paul, and had somehow changed places with *Tally Ho! Songs of Horse and Hound*, which was intended for his mother, and which, unluckily, was a volume of very similar size and shape. Bobby, never losing his head for an instant, explained volubly and in tones of utmost distress to his mother and the company in general that the shop must have sent the wrong book by mistake, and this explanation was rather ungraciously accepted. Greatly to Bobby's disgust, however, *The Sexual Life of Savages in Northern Melanesia* was presently consigned to the stoke-hole flames by Lady Bobbin in person.

The remaining time before dinner, which was early so that the children could come down, was spent by Bobby and Héloïse rushing about the house in a state of wild excitement. Paul suspected, and rightly as it turned out, that this excess of high spirits boded no good to somebody. It was quite obvious to the student of youthful psychology that some practical joke was on hand. He wondered rather nervously where the blow would fall.

It fell during dinner. Captain Chadlington was in the middle of telling Lady Bobbin what the P.M. had said to him about pig-breeding in the West of England when a loud whirring noise was heard under his chair. He looked down, rather startled, turned white to the lips at what he saw, sprang to his feet and said, in a voice of unnatural calm: 'Will the women and children please leave the room immediately. There is an infernal machine under my chair.' A moment of panic ensued. Bobby and Héloïse, almost too swift to apprehend his meaning, rushed to the door shrieking, 'A bomb, a bomb, we shall all be blown up,' while everyone else stood transfixed with horror, looking at the small black box under Captain Chadlington's chair as though uncertain of what they should do next. Paul alone remained perfectly calm. With great presence of mind he advanced towards the box, picked it up and conveyed it to the pantry sink, where he left it with the cold water tap running over it. This golden deed made him, jointly with Captain Chadlington, the hero of the hour. Lady Bobbin shook hands with him and said he was a very plucky young fellow and had saved all their lives, and he was overwhelmed with thanks and praise on every side. Captain Chadlington, too, was supposed to have shown wonderful fortitude in requesting the women and children to leave the room before mentioning his own danger. Only Bobby and Héloïse received no praise from anybody for their behaviour and were, indeed, more or less, sent to Coventry for the rest of the evening.

Captain Chadlington, secretly delighted to think that he was now of such importance politically that attempts were made on his life (he never doubted for a moment that this was the doing of Bolshevik agents) went off to telephone to the police. Bobby and Héloïse, listening round the corner, heard him say: 'Hullo, Woodford police? It is Captain Chadlington, M.P., speaking from Compton Bobbin. Look here, officer, there has just been an attempt to assassinate me. The Bolsheviks, I suppose. An infernal machine under my chair at dinner. Would you send somebody along to examine it at once, please, and inform Scotland Yard of what has happened?'

Lady Brenda said: 'I have always been afraid of something like this ever since Charlie made that speech against Bolshevism at Moreton-in-Marsh. Anyhow, we must be thankful that it was no worse.'

Lady Bobbin said that perhaps now the Government would do something about the Bolsheviks at last.

Lord Leamington Spa said that he didn't like it at all, which was quite true, he didn't, because on Christmas night after dinner he always sang 'The Mistletoe Bough' with great feeling and now it looked as though the others would be too busy talking about the bomb to listen to him.

Michael Lewes and Squibby Almanack dared to wonder whether it was really an infernal machine at all, but they only imparted this scepticism to each other.

The duchess said that of course it would be very good publicity for Charlie Chadlington, and she wondered – but added that perhaps, on the whole, he was too stupid to think of such a thing.

Captain Chadlington said that public men must expect this sort of thing and that he didn't mind for himself, but that it was just like those cowardly dagoes to attempt to blow up a parcel of women and children as well.

Everybody agreed that the tutor had behaved admirably.

'Where did you get it from?' Paul asked Bobby, whom he presently found giggling in the schoolroom with the inevitable Héloïse.

'A boy in my house made it for me last half; he says nobody will be able to tell that it's not a genuine bomb. In fact, it *is* a genuine one, practically; that's the beauty of it. Poor old Charlie Chad., he's most awfully pleased about the whole thing, isn't he, fussing about with those policemen like any old turkey cock. Oh! It all went off too, too beautifully, egI cegouldn't thegink egit fegunnegier, cegould yegou?'

'I think you're an odious child,' said Paul, 'and I've a very good mind to tell your mother about you.'

'That would rather take the gilt off your heroic action, though, wouldn't it, old boy?' said Bobby comfortably.

The local police, as Bobby's friend had truly predicted, were unable to make up their minds as to whether the machine was or was not an infernal one. Until this pretty point should be settled Captain Chadlington was allotted two human bulldogs who were instructed by Scotland Yard that they must guard his life with their own. A camp bed was immediately made up for one of these trusty fellows in the passage, across the captain's bedroom door, and the other was left to prowl about the house and garden all night, armed to the teeth.

'Darling,' said the duchess to Bobby, as they went upstairs to bed after this exhausting day, 'have you seen the lovely man who's sleeping just outside my room? I don't know what your mother expects to happen, but one is only made of flesh and blood after all.'

'Well, for goodness sake, try and remember that you're a duchess again now,' said Bobby, kissing his aunt good night.

J Leech

CHRISTMAS FARE

WASHINGTON IRVING

from 'Old Christmas' in
The Sketch Book of Washington Irving

THE DINNER was served up in the great hall, where the Squire always held his Christmas banquet. A blazing crackling fire of logs had been heaped on to warm the spacious apartment, and the flame went sparkling and wreathing up the wide-mouthed chimney. The great picture of the crusader and his white horse had been profusely decorated with greens for the occasion; and holly and ivy had likewise been wreathed round the helmet and weapons on the opposite wall, which I understood were the arms of the same warrior. I must own, by the by, I had strong doubts about the authenticity of the painting and armour as having belonged to the crusader, they certainly having the stamp of more recent days; but I was told that the painting had been so considered time out of mind; and that as to the armour, it had been found in a lumber room, and elevated to its present situation by the Squire, who at once determined it to be the armour of the family hero; and as he was absolute authority on all such subjects in his own household, the matter had passed into current acceptation. A sideboard was set out just under this chivalric trophy, on which was a display of plate that might have vied (at least in variety) with Belshazzar's parade of the vessels of the temple; 'flagons, cans, cups, beakers, goblets, basins, and ewers'; the gorgeous utensils of good companionship, that had gradually accumulated through many generations of jovial housekeepers. Before these stood the two Yule candles beaming like two stars of the first magnitude; other lights were distributed in branches, and the whole array glittered like a firmament of silver.

We were ushered into this banqueting scene with the sound of minstrelsy, the old harper being seated on a stool beside the fireplace, and twanging his instrument with a vast deal more power than melody. Never did Christmas board display a more goodly and gracious assemblage of countenances: those who were not handsome were, at least, happy; and happiness is a rare improver of your hard-favoured visage. I always consider an old English family as well worth studying as a collection of Holbein's portraits or Albert Durer's prints. There is much antiquarian lore to be acquired; much knowledge of the physiognomies of former times. Perhaps it may be from having continually before their eyes those rows of old family portraits, with which the mansions of this country are stocked; certain it is, that the quaint features of antiquity are often most faithfully perpetuated in these ancient lines; and I have traced an old family nose through a whole picture gallery, legitimately handed down from generation to generation, almost from the time of the Conquest. Something of the kind was to be observed in the worthy company around me. Many of their faces had evidently originated in a Gothic age, and been merely copied by succeeding generations; and there was one little girl, in particular, of staid demeanour, with a high Roman nose, and an antique vinegar aspect, who was a great favourite of the Squire's, being, as he said, a Bracebridge all over, and the very counterpart of one of his ancestors who figured in the court of Henry VIII.

The parson said grace, which was not a short familiar one, such as is commonly addressed to the Deity, in these unceremonious days; but a long, courtly, well-worded one of the ancient school.

There was now a pause, as if something was expected; when suddenly the butler entered the hall with some degree of bustle: he was attended by a servant on each side with a large wax-light, and bore a silver dish, on which was an enormous pig's head decorated with rosemary, with a lemon in its mouth, which was placed with great formality at the head of the table. The moment this pageant made its appearance, the harper struck up a flourish; at the conclusion of which the young Oxonian, on receiving a hint from the Squire, gave, with an air of the most comic gravity, an old carol, the first verse of which was as follows:—

> Caput apri defero
> Reddens laudes Domino.
> The boar's head in hand bring I,
> With garlands gay and rosemary.
> I pray you all synge merily
> Qui estis in convivio.

Though prepared to witness many of these little eccentricities, from being apprised of the peculiar hobby of mine host; yet, I confess, the parade with which so odd a dish was introduced somewhat perplexed me, until I gathered from the conversation of the Squire and the parson that it was meant to represent the bringing in of the boar's head: a dish formerly served up with much ceremony, and the sound of minstrelsy and song, at great tables on Christmas day. 'I like the old custom,' said the Squire, 'not merely because it is stately and pleasing in itself, but because it was observed at the College of Oxford,' at which I was educated. When I hear the old song chanted, it brings to mind the time when I was young and gamesome – and the noble old college-hall – and my fellow students loitering about in their black gowns; many of whom, poor lads, are now in their graves!'

The parson, however, whose mind was not haunted by such associations, and who was always more taken up with the text than the sentiment, objected to the Oxonian's version of the carol; which he affirmed was different from that sung at college. He went on, with the dry perseverance of a commentator, to give the college reading, accompanied by sundry annotations; addressing himself at first to the company at large; but finding their attention gradually diverted to other talk, and other objects, he lowered his tone as his number of auditors diminished, until he concluded his remarks, in an under voice, to a fat-headed old gentleman next him, who was silently engaged in the discussion of a huge plateful of turkey.

The table was literally loaded with good cheer, and presented an epitome of country abundance, in this season of overflowing larders. A distinguished post was allotted to 'ancient sirloin', as mine host termed it; being, as he added, 'the standard of old English hospitality, and a joint of goodly presence, and full of expectation.' There were several dishes quaintly decorated, and which had evidently something traditionary in their embellishments; but about which, as I did not like to appear over-curious, I asked no questions.

I could not, however, but notice a pie, magnificently decorated with peacocks' feathers, in imitation of the tail of that bird, which overshadowed a considerable tract of the table. This the Squire confessed, with some little hesitation, was a pheasant-pie, though a peacock-pie was certainly the most authentical; but there had been such a mortality among the peacocks this season, that he could not prevail upon himself to have one killed.

It would be tedious, perhaps, to my wiser readers, who may not have that foolish fondness for odd and obsolete things to which

I am a little given, were I to mention the other makeshifts of this worthy old humourist, by which he was endeavouring to follow up, though at humble distance, the quaint customs of antiquity. I was pleased, however, to see the respect shown to his whims by his children and relatives; who, indeed, entered readily into the full spirit of them, and seemed all well versed in their parts; having doubtless been present at many a rehearsal. I was amused, too, at the air of profound gravity with which the butler and other servants executed the duties assigned them, however eccentric. They had an old-fashioned look; having, for the most part, been brought up in the household, and grown into keeping with the antiquated mansion, and the humours of its lord; and most probably looked upon all his whimsical regulations as the established laws of honourable housekeeping.

When the cloth was removed, the butler brought in a huge silver vessel of rare and curious workmanship, which he placed before the Squire. Its appearance was hailed with acclamation; being the Wassail Bowl, so renowned in Christmas festivity. The contents had been prepared by the Squire himself; for it was a beverage in the skilful mixture of which he particularly prided himself; alleging that it was too abstruse and complex for the comprehension of an ordinary servant. It was a potation, indeed, that might well make the heart of a toper leap within him; being composed of the richest and raciest wines, highly spiced and sweetened, with roasted apples bobbing about the surface.

The old gentleman's whole countenance beamed with a serene look of indwelling delight, as he stirred this mighty bowl. Having raised it to his lips, with a hearty wish of a merry Christmas to all present, he sent it brimming round the board, for every one to follow his example, according to the primitive style: pronouncing it 'the ancient fountain of good feeling, where all hearts met together'.

There was much laughing and rallying as the honest emblem of Christmas joviality circulated, and was kissed rather coyly by the ladies. When it reached Master Simon he raised it in both hands, and with the air of a boon companion struck up an old Wassail chanson:

> The browne bowle,
> The merry browne bowle,
> As it goes round about-a,
> > Fill
> > Still,
> Let the world say what it will,
> And drink your fill all out-a.

> The deep canne,
> The merry deep canne,
> As thou dost freely quaff-a
> > Sing,
> > Fling,
> Be as merry as a king,
> And sound a lusty laugh-a.

Charles Dickens

from *A Christmas Carol*

SUCH A BUSTLE ensued that you might have thought a goose the rarest of all birds; a feathered phenomenon, to which a black swan was a matter of course – and in truth it was something very like it in that house. Mrs Cratchit made the gravy (ready beforehand in a little saucepan) hissing hot; Master Peter mashed the potatoes with incredible vigour; Miss Belinda sweetened up the apple-sauce; Martha dusted the hot plates; Bob took Tiny Tim beside him in a tiny corner at the table; the two young Cratchits set chairs for everybody, not forgetting themselves, and mounting guard upon their posts, crammed spoons into their mouths, lest they should shriek for goose before their turn came to be helped. At last the dishes were set on and grace was said. It was succeeded by a breathless pause, as Mrs Cratchit, looking slowly all along the carving-knife, prepared to plunge it in the breast; but when she did, and when the long-expected gush of stuffing issued forth, one murmur of delight arose all round the board, and even Tiny Tim, excited by the two young Cratchits, beat on the table with the handle of his knife, and feebly cried Hurrah!

There never was such a goose. Bob said he didn't believe there ever was such a goose cooked. Its tenderness and flavour, size and cheapness, were the themes of universal admiration. Eked out by apple-sauce and mashed potatoes, it was a sufficient dinner for the whole family; indeed, as Mrs Cratchit said with great delight (surveying one small atom of a bone upon the dish), they hadn't ate it all at last! Yet every one had had enough, and the youngest Cratchits in particular, were steeped in sage and onion to the eyebrows! But now, the plates being changed by Miss Belinda, Mrs Cratchit left the room alone – too nervous to bear witnesses – to take the pudding up and bring it in.

Suppose it should not be done enough. Suppose it should break in turning out! Suppose somebody should have got over the wall of the backyard, and stolen it, while they were merry with the goose – a supposition at which the two young Cratchits became livid. All sorts of horrors were supposed.

Hallo! A great deal of steam! The pudding was out of the copper. A smell like a washing-day! That was the cloth. A smell like an eating-house and a pastry-cook's next door to each other, with a laundress's next door to that! That was the pudding! In half a minute Mrs Cratchit entered – flushed, but smiling proudly – with the pudding, like a speckled cannon-ball, so hard and firm, blazing in half of half-a-quartern of ignited brandy, and bedight with Christmas holly stuck into the top.

Oh, a wonderful pudding! Bob Cratchit said, and calmly too, that he regarded it as the greatest success achieved by Mrs Cratchit since their marriage. Mrs Cratchit said, that now the weight was off her mind, she would confess she had had her doubts about the quantity of flour. Everybody had something to say about it, but nobody said or thought it was at all a small pudding for a large family. It would have been flat heresy to do so. Any Cratchit would have blushed to hint at such a thing.

At last the dinner was all done, the cloth was cleared, the hearth swept, and the fire made up. The compound in the jug being tasted, and considered perfect, apples and oranges were put upon the table, and a shovel full of chestnuts on the fire. Then all the Cratchit family drew round the hearth, in what Bob Cratchit called a circle, meaning half a one, and at Bob Cratchit's elbow stood the family display of glass – two tumblers and a custard-cup without a handle.

These held the hot stuff from the jug, however, as well as golden goblets would have done; and Bob served it out with beaming looks, while the chestnuts on the fire sputtered and cracked noisily. Then Bob proposed:

'A Merry Christmas to us all, my dears. God bless us!'

Which all the family re-echoed.

'God bless us every one!' said Tiny Tim, the last of all.

Thomas Tusser

Christmas Husbandly Fare from
Five Hundred Pointes of Good Husbandrie

Good husband and huswife, now chiefly be glad,
things handsome to have, as they ought to be had.
They both do provide, against Christmas do come,
to welcom their neighbors, good cheer to have some.

Good bread and good drinke, a good fier in the hall,
brawne, pudding, and souse, and good mustarde withal.
Beef, mutton, and Porke, and good Pies of the best,
pig, veale, goose, and capon, and turkey wel drest,
Cheese, apples and nuttes, and good Caroles to heare,
as then, in the cuntrey is counted good cheare.

What cost to good husbande, is any of this?
good householde provision onely it is:
Of other the like, I do leave out a meny,
that costeth the husband never a peny.

Benjamin Zephaniah

Talking Turkeys!!

Be nice to yu turkeys dis christmas
Cos turkeys jus wanna hav fun
Turkeys are cool, turkeys are wicked
An every turkey has a Mum.
Be nice to yu turkeys dis christmas,
Don't eat it, keep it alive,
It could be yu mate an not on yu plate
Say, Yo! Turkey I'm on your side.

I got lots of friends who are turkeys
An all of dem fear christmas time,
Dey wanna enjoy it, dey say humans destroyed it
An humans are out of dere mind,
Yeah, I got lots of friends who are turkeys
Dey all hav a right to a life,
Not to be caged up an genetically made up
By any farmer an his wife.

Turkeys just wanna play reggae
Turkeys just wanna hip-hop
Can yu imagine a nice young turkey saying,
'I cannot wait for de chop'?
Turkeys like getting presents, dey wanna watch christmas TV,
Turkeys hav brains an turkeys feel pain
In many ways like yu an me.

I once knew a turkey called Turkey
He said 'Benji explain to me please,
Who put de turkey in christmas
An what happens to christmas trees?'
I said, 'I am not too sure turkey
But it's nothing to do wid Christ Mass
Humans get greedy an waste more dan need be
An business men mek loadsa cash'.

Be nice to yu turkey dis christmas
Invite dem indoors fe sum greens
Let dem eat cake an let dem partake
In a plate of organic grown beans,
Be nice to yu turkey dis christmas
An spare dem de cut of de knife,
Join Turkeys United an dey'll be delighted
An yu will mek new friends 'FOR LIFE'.

P.G. Wodehouse

Another Christmas Carol

The subject of dieting had come up in the bar-parlour of the Anglers' Rest, and a thoughtful Gin and Tonic said he wondered how fellows who were on a diet managed at Christmas.

'Precisely the problem which presented itself to my cousin Egbert,' said Mr Mulliner.

'Was he on a diet?' a Scotch on the Rocks asked.

Very much the reverse (continued Mr Mulliner) until one day he felt a funny feeling in the upper left side of his chest and went to see a medical friend of his, a Dr Potter.

'And what can I do for you, L. Nero Wolfe?' said Dr Potter.

It was a sobriquet which had been bestowed on my cousin at their mutual school, for even then his ample frame had invited criticism. Egbert had started life as a bouncing baby, had grown into a bulbous boy, and was now, in his forty-second year, a man beneath whom weighing machines quivered like aspens. In common with all his ancestors he had a passionate love of food, but while they had worked off their superfluous tissue by jousting, fighting the Paynim, dancing old English dances and what not, on him it had accumulated.

'I don't think it's anything much, Bill,' he replied, 'but I thought I had better get a medical opinion. It's a sort of pain ... well, not a pain exactly, more of a kind of funny feeling up here on the left side of my chest. It catches me when I breathe.'

'Don't breathe,' said Dr Potter, for it was Christmas time, when even Harley Street physicians like their little joke. 'All right, let's have a look at you. ... H'm,' he said, the examination concluded. 'Ha,' he added, and threw in another 'H'm' for good measure. 'Yes, just as I supposed. You're too fat.'

This surprised Egbert. He had sometimes thought that he might be an ounce or two overweight, but he would never have applied such an adjective to himself.

'Would you call me fat?'

'I'd go further. I'd call you grossly obese, and the fat's accumulating round your heart. We'll have to get at least a stone off you. If we don't –'

'What happens if we don't?'

'All that fuss and bother of buying wreaths and turning out for your funeral.'

'Good heavens, Bill!'

'It's no use saying "Good heavens". For a year you've got to knock off all starchy foods, all rich foods. In fact it wouldn't be a bad idea if you knocked off food altogether.'

It was a crushing blow, but there was good stuff in Egbert Mulliner. Though nothing could make such a régime agreeable, he was confident that he could go through with it. It was not as if he were not used to roughing it. He had often been at cocktail parties where the supply of sausages on those little wooden sticks had given out, and a sort of reserve strength had pulled him through.

His upper lip was stiff as he left the consulting room. It remained so till he was in the street, when all the stiffening suddenly went out of it. He had remembered his Aunt Serena, with whom as usual he would be taking dinner on the night of Christmas Day.

85

As Egbert from boyhood up had shown no signs of possessing any intelligence whatsoever, a place had been found for him in the Civil Service. But though he could drink tea at four o'clock as well as the next man, he had not really liked being in his country's service, however civil. What he wanted was to buy a partnership in a friend's interior decorating and antique selling firm, and this could be done only if his Aunt Serena, who was extraordinarily rich, put up the money. He had often asked her to do so and she had refused because she thought that haggling with customers about prices would bruise his gentle spirit. He had planned to make one last appeal on Christmas night when she would be mellowed by food and drink.

But in what frame of mind would a touchy hostess, who prided herself on the lavishness of her hospitality, be to finance a nephew who refused every course of the dinner she had taken such pains to assemble?

Two minutes later he was back in Dr Potter's consulting room.

'Listen, Bill,' he said. 'You were only kidding just now about that diet, weren't you?'

'I was not.'

'What would happen if I ate caviar, turtle soup, turkey, plum pudding, mince pies, biscuit tortoni, hot rolls with butter and crystallized fruit and drank hock, champagne, port and liqueurs. Would I die?'

'Of course. But what a jolly death. Were you thinking of doing that?'

'It's what I shall have to do when I have Christmas dinner at my aunt's. If I skip a single course, she will never speak to me again, and bang will go my interior decorator partnership,' said Egbert, and in the clear concise way civil servants have he explained the delicate position in which he found himself.

Dr Potter listened attentively and at the conclusion of the narrative said 'H'm,' added 'Ha,' and then said 'H'm' again.

'You're sure that abstinence on your part would offend this aunt of whom you speak?'

'She would never forgive me.'

'Then you must get out of it.'

'I can't get out of it.'

'You could if you had a good excuse. She could hardly blame you if, for instance, you had bubonic plague. I could inject a serum into you which would give you all the bubonic plague a heart could desire.'

Egbert weighed the suggestion. He appreciated its ingenuity, but nevertheless he hesitated.

'What's bubonic plague like?'

'I don't know that it's like anything. Except, of course, bubonic plague.'

'Is it painful?'

'I've never had it myself, but I'm told it gives you a sort of funny feeling.'

'Don't you come out in spots?'

'I believe that is the usual procedure.'

Egbert shook his head.

'I don't think I'll have it.'

'Then have an accident.'

'What sort of accident?'

'The choice is wide, but perhaps the simplest thing would be to get run over by a taxi cab.'

'Have you ever been run over by a taxi cab?'

'Dozens of times.'

'Did it hurt?'

'Just a kind of tickling sensation.'

Egbert mused a while.

'That does seem the best thing to do.'

'Much the best.'

'And there's no need to get actually run over. I can just step off into the road and stick a leg out.'

'Exactly. The charioteer will do the rest.'

Christmas Day dawned with its sprinkling of snow, its robin red-breasts and all the things one has always been led to expect, and as it progressed Egbert's determination to follow the doctor's advice became solidified. He was not altogether persuaded of the accuracy of the latter's statement that getting together with a taxi cab caused merely a kind of tickling sensation, but even if the results were far worse, they must be faced. As he walked up to his aunt's house, he was encouraged to see there was no stint of the necessary vehicles. They whizzed to and fro in dozens, and to extend a leg in front of one of them would be a task well within the scope of the least gifted man. It was simply a matter of making one's selection.

He rejected the first that came along because he disliked the driver's moustache, the second because the cab was the wrong colour, and he was just about to step in front of a third which met all his qualifications, when he paused with leg in air. He had suddenly remembered that his aunt's birthday was on February the eleventh, by which time he would be out of hospital and expected as a guest at the banquet with which she always celebrated her natal day. And her birthday dinners, as he knew full well, were just as stupendous as those at Christmas.

Of course, it would be open to him to get knocked down by another taxi cab on February the tenth but if he yielded to this temptation, how would his superiors at the office react? Would they not shake their heads and say to one another 'Mulliner has got into a rut' and feel that the services of an employee so accident prone were better dispensed with?

It was a possibility that froze his feet and caused both his chins to tremble. The salary the taxpayers paid him for drinking tea at four o'clock was not as generous as he could have wished, but it was all he had. Bereft of it, he would be penniless. And he would not even be able to beg his bread in the streets, for his medical adviser had expressly forbidden him all starchy foods.

Only one course lay before him. Whatever the price involved, he must continue on his way to his aunt's residence and there tuck, though with a heavy heart, into the caviar, the turtle soup, the turkey, the plum pudding, the mince pies, the biscuit tortoni, the hot rolls with butter and the crystallized fruit, washing them down with hock, champagne, port and liqueurs. If the worst happened, he reflected, for he was a philosophical man, it would be just one more grave among the hills. Nevertheless, though philosophical, it was in no buoyant mood that he came to journey's end and exchanged Christmas greetings with his aunt in her ornate drawing room. There was, he noted, even more of her than when they had last met. She, too, had started life as a bouncing baby and from there had grown into a globular girl, finishing up as one of the three stoutest women in the W1 postal division of London.

He delivered his Christmas gift, and in return she pressed into his hand an oblong slip of paper.

'The money for your partnership, dear,' she said.

It would have seemed incredible to anyone, seeing Egbert, that he was capable of swelling with ecstasy any more than he was swelling already, but at these words he seemed to expand like one of those odd circular fish you get down in Florida, which when hauled to the surface puff themselves out like balloons. His nose quivered, his ears wiggled, his eyes, usually devoid of any expression whatsoever, shone like twin stars. He had not felt such a gush of elation since his seventh birthday, when somebody had given him a box of chocolates and he had devoured the top layer and supposed that that was the end and then had found that there was a second layer lurking underneath. He put his arm round his aunt's waist as far as it would go, and kissed her fondly.

'How can I thank you?' he murmured brokenly.

'I thought you would be pleased, dear,' she said. 'But now I am afraid I have a little disappointment for you. Do you read a magazine called *Pure Diet and World Redemption*?'

'Is that the one that has all those pictures of girls without any clothes on?'

'No, that is *Playboy*. I subscribe to that regularly. This one is all about vegetarianism. A copy was left here by mistake last week. I glanced at it idly, and my whole outlook became changed. It said vegetarianism was an absolute vital essential prerequisite to a new order of civilization in which humanity will have become truly humane.'

Egbert, as far as was possible for one of his stoutness, leapt in his chair. A wild thought had flashed into his mind, such as it was. Not even if he had been a victim of bubonic plague could the feeling he was feeling have been funnier.

'Do you mean –?'

'It said that only thus can there come peace on earth with

a cessation of wars, the abolition of crime, diseases, insanity, poverty and oppression. And you can't say that wouldn't be nice, can you dear?'

As a rule, Egbert when speaking had the beautifully clear enunciation found only in the Civil Service, but now emotion made him stutter.

'Do you mean,' he cried, inserting five or six m's into the last word, 'that you have become a vegetarian?'

'Yes, dear.'

'There won't be any turkey tonight?'

'I'm afraid not.'

'No turtle soup? No mince pies?'

'I know how disappointed you must be.'

Egbert, who had leapt in his chair, sprang from it like some lissom adagio dancer, a feat against the performance of which any knowledgeable bookmaker would have given odds of at least a hundred to eight.

'Disappointed?' he thundered. 'Disappointed? I couldn't be more pleased. I've just become a vegetarian myself. Well, practically. I wouldn't touch a turkey with a ten-foot pole. What shall we be having for dinner?'

'To start with, seaweed soup.'

'Most nutritious.'

'Then mock salmon. It is vegetable marrow coloured pink.'

'Splendid!'

'Followed by nut cutlets with spinach.'

'Capital!'

'And an orange.'

'We split one?'

'No, one each.'

'A positive banquet. God bless us, every one,' said Egbert.

He had a feeling that he had heard that before somewhere, but we cannot all be original, and it seemed to him to sum up the situation about as neatly as a situation could be summed up.

CHRISTMAS AT WAR

Christmas Bells

I heard the bells on Christmas Day
    Their old familiar carols play,
      And wild and sweet
      The words repeat
Of peace on earth, good-will to men!

And thought how, as the day had come,
The belfries of all Christendom
      Had rolled along
      The unbroken song
Of peace on earth, good-will to men!

Till, ringing, singing on its way,
The world revolved from night to day,
      A voice, a chime
      A chant sublime
Of peace on earth, good-will to men!

Then from each black accursed mouth
The cannon thundered in the South,
      And with the sound
      The carols drowned
Of peace on earth, good-will to men!

It was as if an earthquake rent
The hearth-stones of a continent,
   And made forlorn
   The households born
Of peace on earth, good-will to men!

And in despair I bowed my head;
'There is no peace on earth,' I said;
   'For hate is strong,
   And mocks the song
Of peace on earth, good-will to men!'

Then pealed the bells more loud and deep:
'God is not dead; nor doth he sleep!
   The Wrong shall fail,
   The Right prevail,
With peace on earth, good-will to men!'

THOMAS HARDY

A Christmas Ghost-Story

South of the Line, inland from far Durban,
A mouldering soldier lies – your countryman.
Awry and doubled up are his gray bones,
And on the breeze his puzzled phantom moans
Nightly to clear Canopus: 'I would know
By whom and when the All-Earth-gladdening Law
Of Peace, brought in by that Man Crucified,
Was ruled to be inept, and set aside?
And what of logic or of truth appears
In tacking 'Anno Domini' to the years?
Near twenty-hundred liveried thus have hied,
But tarries yet the Cause for which He died.'

Christmas Eve, 1899

Cyril Winterbotham

A Christmas Prayer

FROM THE TRENCHES

Not yet for us may Christmas bring
   Good-will to men, and peace;
In our dark sky no angels sing,
   Not yet the great release
   For men, when war shall cease.

So must the guns our carols make,
   Our gifts must bullets be,
For us no Christmas bells shall wake;
   These ruined homes shall see
   No Christmas revelry.

In hardened hearts we fain would greet
   The Babe at Christmas born,
But lo, He comes with piercèd feet,
   Wearing a crown of thorn, –
   His side a spear has torn.

For tired eyes are all too dim,
   Our hearts too full of pain,
Our ears too deaf to hear the hymn
   Which angels sing in vain,
   'The Christ is born again'.

O Jesus, pitiful, draw near,
    That even we may see
The Little Child who knew not fear;
    Thus would we picture Thee
    Unmarred by agony.

O'er death and pain triumphant yet
    Bid Thou Thy harpers play,
That we may hear them, and forget
    Sorrow and all dismay,
    And welcome Thee to stay
    With us on Christmas Day.

G.K. CHESTERTON

The Truce of Christmas

Passionate peace is in the sky —
And in the snow in silver sealed
The beasts are perfect in the field,
And men seem men so suddenly —
   (But take ten swords and ten times ten
   And blow the bugle in praising men;
   For we are for all men under the sun,
   And they are against us every one;
   And misers haggle and madmen clutch,
   And there is peril in praising much.
   And we have the terrible tongues uncurled
   That praise the world to the sons of the world.)

The idle humble hill and wood
Are bowed upon the sacred birth,
And for one little hour the earth
Is lazy with the love of good —
   (But ready are you, and ready am I,
   If the battle blow and the guns go by;
   For we are for all men under the sun,
   And they are against us every one;
   And the men that hate herd all together,
   To pride and gold, and the great white feather,
   And the thing is graven in star and stone
   That the men who love are all alone.)

Hunger is hard and time is tough,
But bless the beggars and kiss the kings,
For hope has broken the heart of things,
And nothing was ever praised enough.
    (But bold the shield for a sudden swing
    And point the sword when you praise a thing,
    For we are for all men under the sun,
    And they are against us every one;
    And mime and merchant, thane and thrall
    Hate us because we love them all;
    Only till Christmastide go by
    Passionate peace is in the sky.)

W.H. DAVIES

The Holly on the Wall

Play, little children, one and all,
For holly, holly on the wall.
You do not know that millions are
This moment in a deadly war;
Millions of men whose Christmas bells
Are guns' reports and bursting shells;
Whose holly berries, made of lead,
Take human blood to stain them red;
Whose leaves are swords, and bayonets too,
To pierce their fellow-mortals through.
For now the war is here, and men –
Like cats that stretch their bodies when
The light has gone and darkness comes –
Have armed and left their peaceful homes:
But men will be, when there's no war,
As gentle as you children are.
Play, little children, one and all,
For holly, holly on the wall.

A CHILD'S CHRISTMAS

Dylan Thomas

from *A Child's Christmas in Wales*

ONE CHRISTMAS was so much like another, in those years around the sea-town corner now and out of all sound except the distant speaking of the voices I sometimes hear a moment before sleep, that I can never remember whether it snowed for six days and six nights when I was twelve or whether it snowed for twelve days and twelve nights when I was six.

All the Christmases roll down toward the two-tongued sea, like a cold and headlong moon bundling down the sky that was our street; and they stop at the rim of the ice-edged, fish-freezing waves, and I plunge my hands in the snow and bring out whatever I can find. In goes my hand into that wool-white bell-tongued ball of holidays resting at the rim of the carol-singing sea, and out come Mrs Prothero and the firemen.

It was on the afternoon of the day of Christmas Eve, and I was in Mrs Prothero's garden, waiting for cats, with her son Jim. It was snowing. It was always snowing at Christmas. December, in my memory, is white as Lapland, though there were no reindeers. But there were cats. Patient, cold and callous, our hands wrapped in socks, we waited to snowball the cats. Sleek and long as jaguars and horrible-whiskered, spitting and snarling, they would slink and sidle over the white back-garden walls, and the lynx-eyed hunters, Jim and I, fur-capped and moccasined trappers from Hudson Bay, off Mumbles Road, would hurl our deadly snowballs at the green of their eyes.

The wise cats never appeared. We were so still, Eskimo-footed arctic marksmen in the muffling silence of the eternal snows – eternal, ever since Wednesday – that we never heard Mrs Prothero's first cry from her igloo at the bottom of the garden. Or, if we heard it at all, it was, to us, like the far-off challenge of our enemy and prey, the neighbour's polar cat. But soon the voice grew louder. 'Fire!' cried Mrs Prothero, and she beat the dinner-gong.

And we ran down the garden, with the snowballs in our arms, toward the house; and smoke, indeed, was pouring out of the dining-room, and the gong was bombilating, and Mrs Prothero was announcing ruin like a town crier in Pompeii. This was better than all the cats in Wales standing on the wall in a row. We bounded into the house, laden with snowballs, and stopped at the open door of the smoke-filled room.

Something was burning all right; perhaps it was Mr Prothero, who always slept there after midday dinner with a newspaper over his face. But he was standing in the middle of the room, saying, 'A fine Christmas!' and smacking at the smoke with a slipper. 'Call the fire brigade,' cried Mrs Prothero as she beat the gong.

'They won't be there,' said Mr Prothero, 'it's Christmas.'

There was no fire to be seen, only clouds of smoke and Mr Prothero standing in the middle of them, waving his slipper as though he were conducting.

'Do something,' he said.

And we threw all our snowballs into the smoke – I think we missed Mr Prothero – and ran out of the house to the telephone box.

'Let's call the police as well,' Jim said.

'And the ambulance.'

'And Ernie Jenkins, he likes fires.'

But we only called the fire brigade, and soon the fire engine came and three tall men in helmets brought a hose into the house and Mr Prothero got out just in time before they turned it on. Nobody could have had a noisier Christmas Eve. And when the firemen turned off the hose and were standing in the wet, smoky room, Jim's aunt, Miss Prothero, came downstairs and peered in at them. Jim and I waited, very quietly, to hear what she would say to them. She said the right thing, always. She looked at the three tall firemen in their shining helmets, standing among the smoke and cinders and dissolving snowballs, and she said, 'Would you like anything to read?'

KENNETH GRAHAME

from *The Wind in the Willows*

'WHAT A CAPITAL little house this is!' [the Rat] called out cheerily. 'So compact! So well planned! Everything here and everything in its place! We'll make a jolly night of it. The first thing we want is a good fire; I'll see to that – I always know where to find things. So this is the parlour? Splendid! Your own idea, those little sleeping-bunks in the wall? Capital! Now, I'll fetch the wood and the coals, and you get a duster, Mole – you'll find one in the drawer of the kitchen table – and try and smarten things up a bit. Bustle about, old chap!'

Encouraged by his inspiriting companion, the Mole roused himself and dusted and polished with energy and heartiness, while the Rat, running to and fro with armfuls of fuel, soon had a cheerful blaze roaring up the chimney. He hailed the Mole to come and warm himself; but Mole promptly had another fit of the blues, dropping down on a couch in dark despair and burying his face in his duster.

'Rat,' he moaned, 'how about your supper, you poor, cold, hungry, weary animal? I've nothing to give you – nothing – not a crumb!'

'What a fellow you are for giving in!' said the Rat reproachfully. 'Why, only just now I saw a sardine-opener on the kitchen dresser, quite distinctly; and everybody knows that means there are sardines about somewhere in the neighbourhood. Rouse yourself! pull yourself together, and come with me and forage.'

They went and foraged accordingly, hunting through every cupboard and turning out every drawer. The result was not so very depressing after all, though of course it might have been better; a tin of sardines – a box of captain's biscuits, nearly full – and a German sausage encased in silver paper.

'There's a banquet for you!' observed the Rat, as he arranged the table. 'I know some animals who would give their ears to be sitting down to supper with us to-night!'

'No bread!' groaned the Mole dolorously; 'no butter, no ——'

'No *pâté de foie gras*, no champagne!' continued the Rat, grinning. 'And that reminds me – what's that little door at the end of the passage? Your cellar, of course! Every luxury in this house! Just you wait a minute.'

He made for the cellar-door, and presently reappeared, somewhat dusty, with a bottle of beer in each paw and another under each arm, 'Self-indulgent beggar you seem to be, Mole,' he observed. 'Deny yourself nothing. This is really the jolliest little place I ever was in. Now, wherever did you pick up those prints? Make the place look so home-like, they do. No wonder you're so fond of it, Mole. Tell us all about it, and how you came to make it what it is.'

Then, while the Rat busied himself fetching plates, and knives and forks, and mustard which he mixed in an egg-cup, the Mole, his bosom still heaving with the stress of his recent emotion, related – somewhat shyly at first, but with more freedom as he warmed to his subject – how this was planned, and how that was thought out, and how this was got through a windfall from an aunt, and that was a wonderful find and a bargain, and this other thing was bought out of laborious savings and a certain amount of 'going without'. His spirits finally quite restored, he

108

must needs go and caress his possessions, and take a lamp and show off their points to his visitor and expatiate on them, quite forgetful of the supper they both so much needed; Rat, who was desperately hungry but strove to conceal it, nodding seriously, examining with a puckered brow, and saying, 'Wonderful,' and 'Most remarkable,' at intervals, when the chance for an observation was given him.

At last the Rat succeeded in decoying him to the table, and had just got seriously to work with the sardine-opener when sounds were heard from the fore-court without – sounds like the scuffling of small feet in the gravel and a confused murmur of tiny voices, while broken sentences reached them – 'Now, all in a line – hold the lantern up a bit, Tommy – clear your throats first – no coughing after I say one, two, three. – Where's young Bill? – Here, come on, do, we're all a-waiting—'

'What's up?' inquired the Rat, pausing in his labours.

'I think it must be the field-mice,' replied the Mole, with a touch of pride in his manner. 'They go round carol-singing regularly at this time of the year. They're quite an institution in these parts. And they never pass me over – they come to Mole End last of all; and I used to give them hot drinks, and supper too sometimes, when I could afford it. It will be like old times to hear them again.'

'Let's have a look at them!' cried the Rat, jumping up and running to the door.

It was a pretty sight, and a seasonable one, that met their eyes when they flung the door open. In the fore-court, lit by the dim rays of a horn lantern, some eight or ten little field-mice stood in a semicircle, red worsted comforters round their throats, their fore-paws thrust deep into their pockets, their feet jigging for warmth. With bright beady eyes they glanced shyly at each other, sniggering a little, sniffing and applying coat-sleeves a good deal. As the door opened, one of the elder ones that carried the lantern was just saying, 'Now then, one, two, three!' and forthwith their shrill little voices uprose on the air, singing one of the old-time carols that their forefathers composed in fields that were fallow and held by frost, or when snow-bound in chimney corners, and handed down to be sung in the miry street to lamp-lit windows at Yule-time.

CAROL

Villagers all, this frosty tide,
Let your doors swing open wide,
Though wind may follow, and snow beside,
Yet draw us in by your fire to bide;
Joy shall be yours in the morning!

Here we stand in the cold and the sleet,
Blowing fingers and stamping feet,
Come from far away you to greet —
You by the fire and we in the street —
Bidding you joy in the morning!

For ere one half of the night was gone,
Sudden a star has led us on,
Raining bliss and benison —
Bliss to-morrow and more anon,
Joy for every morning!

Goodman Joseph toiled through the snow —
Saw the star o'er a stable low;
Mary she might not further go —
Welcome thatch, and litter below!
Joy was hers in the morning!

And then they heard the angels tell
'Who were the first to cry Nowell?
Animals all, as it befell,
In the stable where they did dwell!
Joy shall be theirs in the morning!'

RICHARD MIDDLETON

The Carol of the Poor Children

We are the poor children, come out to see the sights
On this day of all days, on this night of nights,
The stars in merry parties are dancing in the sky,
A fine star, a new star, is shining on high!

We are the poor children, our lips are frosty blue,
We cannot sing our carol as well as rich folk do,
Our bellies are so empty we have no singing voice,
But this night of all nights good children must rejoice.

We do rejoice, we do rejoice, as hard as we can try,
A fine star, a new star is shining in the sky!
And while we sing our carol, we think of the delight
The happy kings and shepherds make in Bethlehem to-night.

Are we naked, mother, and are we starving poor –
Oh, see what gifts the kings have brought outside the stable
    door,
Are we cold, mother, the ass will give his hay
To make the manger warm and keep the cruel winds away.

We are the poor children, but not so poor who sing
Our carol with our voiceless hearts to greet the new-born king,
On this night of all nights, when in the frosty sky
A new star, a kind star is shining on high!

LOUISA MAY ALCOTT

from *Little Women*

JO WAS THE FIRST to wake in the grey dawn of Christmas morning. No stockings hung at the fireplace, and for a moment she felt as much disappointed as she did long ago, when her little sock fell down because it was so crammed with goodies. Then she remembered her mother's promise, and, slipping her hand under her pillow, drew out a little crimson-covered book. She knew it very well, for it was that beautiful old story of the best life ever lived, and Jo felt that it was a true guide-book for any pilgrim going the long journey. She woke Meg with a 'Merry Christmas', and bade her see what was under her pillow. A green-covered book appeared, with the same picture inside, and a few words written by their mother, which made their one present very precious in their eyes. Presently Beth and Amy woke to rummage and find their little books also – one dove-coloured, the other blue; and all sat looking at and talking about them, while the east grew rosy with the coming day.

In spite of her small vanities, Margaret had a sweet and pious nature, which unconsciously influenced her sisters, especially Jo, who loved her very tenderly, and obeyed her because her advice was so gently given.

'Girls,' said Meg seriously, looking from the tumbled head beside her to the two little night-capped ones in the room beyond, 'mother wants us to read and love and mind these books, and we must begin at once. We used to be faithful about it; but since father went away and all this war trouble unsettled us, we have neglected many things. You can do as you please, but *I* shall keep my book on the table here and read a little every morning as soon as I wake, for I know it will do me good and help me through the day.'

Then she opened her new book and began to read. Jo put her arm round her and, leaning cheek to cheek, read also, with the quiet expression so seldom seen on her restless face.

'How good Meg is! Come, Amy, let's do as they do. I'll help you with the hard words, and they'll explain things if we don't understand,' whispered Beth, very much impressed by the pretty books and her sisters' example.

'I'm glad mine is blue,' said Amy; and then the rooms were very still while the pages were softly turned, and the winter sunshine crept in to touch the bright heads and serious faces with a Christmas greeting.

'Where is Mother?' asked Meg, as she and Jo ran down to thank her for their gifts, half an hour later.

'Goodness only knows. Some poor creeter came a-beggin', and your ma went straight off to see what was needed. There never *was* such a woman for givin' away vittles and drink, clothes and firin',' replied Hannah, who had lived with the family since Meg was born, and was considered by them all more as a friend than a servant.

'She will be back soon, I think, so fry your cake, and have everything ready,' said Meg, looking over the presents which were collected in a basket and kept under the sofa, ready to be produced at the proper time. 'Why, where is Amy's bottle of cologne?' she added, as the little flask did not appear.

'She took it out a minute ago, and went off with it to put a ribbon on it, or some such notion,' replied Jo, dancing about the room to take the first stiffness off the new army slippers.

'How nice my handkerchiefs look, don't they? Hannah washed and ironed them for me, and I marked them all myself,' said Beth, looking proudly at the somewhat uneven letters which had cost her such labour.

'Bless the child! She's gone and put "Mother" on them instead of "M. March". How funny!' cried Jo, taking up one.

'Isn't that right? I thought it was better to do it so, because Meg's initials are "M.M.", and I don't want anyone to use these but Marmee,' said Beth, looking troubled.

'It's all right, dear, and a very pretty idea – quite sensible, too, for no one can ever mistake now. It will please her very much, I know,' said Meg, with a frown for Jo and a smile for Beth.

'There's Mother. Hide the basket, quick!' cried Jo, as a door slammed and steps sounded in the hall.

Amy came in hastily, and looked rather abashed when she saw her sisters all waiting for her.

'Where have you been, and what are you hiding behind you?' asked Meg, surprised to see, by her hood and cloak, that lazy Amy had been out so early.

'Don't laugh at me, Jo! I didn't mean anyone should know till the time came. I only meant to change the little bottle for a big one, and I gave *all* my money to get it, and I'm truly trying not to be selfish any more.'

As she spoke, Amy showed the handsome flask which replaced the cheap one, and looked so earnest and humble in her little effort to forget herself that Meg hugged her on the spot, and Jo pronounced her 'a trump', while Beth ran to the window and picked her finest rose to ornament the stately bottle.

'You see, I felt ashamed of my present, after reading and talking about being good this morning, so I ran round the corner and changed it the minute I was up; and I'm *so* glad, for mine is the handsomest now.'

Another bang of the street door sent the basket under the sofa, and the girls to the table, eager for breakfast.

'Merry Christmas, Marmee! Many of them! Thank you for our books. We read some, and mean to, every day,' they cried, in chorus.

'Merry Christmas, little daughters! I'm glad you began at once, and hope you will keep on. But I want to say one word before we sit down. Not far away from here lies a poor woman with a little new-born baby. Six children are huddled into one bed to keep from freezing, for they have no fire. There is nothing to eat over there, and the oldest boy came to tell me they were suffering hunger and cold. My girls, will you give them your breakfast as a Christmas present?'

They were all unusually hungry, having waited nearly an hour, and for a minute no one spoke; only a minute, for Jo exclaimed impetuously –

'I'm so glad you came before we began!'

'May I go and help carry the things to the poor little children?' asked Beth eagerly.

'*I* shall take the cream and the muffins,' added Amy, heroically, giving up the article she most liked.

Meg was already covering the buckwheats, and piling the bread into one big plate.

'I thought you'd do it,' said Mrs March, smiling as if satisfied. 'You shall all go and help me, and when we come back we will have bread and milk for breakfast, and make it up at dinner-time.'

They were soon ready, and the procession set out. Fortunately it was early, and they went through back streets, so few people saw them, and no one laughed at the queer party.

A poor, bare, miserable room it was, with broken windows, no fire, ragged bed-clothes, a sick mother, wailing baby, and a group of pale, hungry children cuddled under one old quilt, trying to keep warm.

How the big eyes stared and the blue lips smiled as the girls went in!

'Ach, mein Gott! It is good angels come to us!' said the poor woman, crying for joy.

'Funny angels in hoods and mittens,' said Jo, and set them laughing.

In a few minutes it really did seem as if kind spirits had been at work there. Hannah, who had carried wood, made a fire, and stopped up the broken panes with old hats and her own cloak. Mrs March gave the mother tea and gruel, and comforted her with promises of help, while she dressed the little baby as tenderly as if it had been her own. The girls, meantime, spread the table, set the children round the fire, and fed them like so many hungry birds – laughing, talking, and trying to understand the funny broken English.

'Das ist gut!' 'Die Engel-kinder!' cried the poor things, as they ate and warmed their purple hands at the comfortable blaze.

The girls had never been called angel children before, and thought it very agreeable, especially Jo, who had been considered a 'Sancho' ever since she was born. That was a very happy breakfast, though they didn't get any of it. And when they went away, leaving comfort behind, I think there were not in all the city four merrier people than the hungry little girls who gave away their breakfasts and contented themselves with bread and milk on Christmas morning.

George Mackay Brown

The Lost Boy

THERE WAS ONE light in the village on Christmas Eve; it came from Jock Scabra's cottage, and he was the awkwardest old man that had ever lived in our village or in the island, or in the whole of Orkney.

I was feeling very wretched and very ill-natured myself that evening. My Aunty Belle had just been explaining to me after tea that Santa Claus, if he did exist, was a spirit that moved people's hearts to generosity and goodwill; no more or less.

Gone was my fat apple-cheeked red-coated friend of the past ten winters. Scattered were the reindeer, broken the sledge that had beaten such a marvellous path through the constellations and the Merry Dancers, while all the children of Orkney slept. Those merry perilous descents down the lum, Yule eve by Yule eve, with the sack of toys and books, games and chocolate boxes, had never really taken place at all…I looked over towards our hearth, after my aunt had finished speaking: the magic had left it, it was only a place of peat flames and peat smoke.

I can't tell you how angry I was, the more I thought about it. How deceitful, how cruel, grown-ups were! They had exiled my dear old friend, Santa Claus, to eternal oblivion. The gifts I would find in my stocking next morning would have issued from Aunty Belle's 'spirit of generosity'. It was not the same thing at all. (Most of the year I saw little enough of that spirit of generosity – at Halloween, for example, she had boxed my ears till I saw stars

118

that had never been in the sky, for stealing a few apples and nuts out of the cupboard, before 'dooking' time.)

If there was a more ill-tempered person than my Aunty Belle in the village, it was, as I said, old Jock Scabra, the fisherman with a silver ring in his ear and a fierce one-eyed tom cat.

His house, alone in the village, was lit that night. I saw it, from our own front door, at eleven o'clock.

Aunty Belle's piece of common sense had so angered me, that I was in a state of rebellion and recklessness. No, I would *not* sleep. I would not even stay in a house from which Santa had been banished. I felt utterly betrayed and bereaved.

When, about half past ten, I heard rending snores coming from Aunty Belle's bedroom, I got out of bed stealthily and put my cold clothes on, and unlatched the front door and went outside. The whole house had betrayed me – well, I intended to be out of the treacherous house when the magic hour of midnight struck.

The road through the village was deep in snow, dark except where under old Scabra's window the lamplight had stained it an orange colour. The snow shadows were blue under his walls. The stars were like sharp nails. Even though I had wrapped my scarf twice round my neck, I shivered in the bitter night.

Where could I go? The light in the old villain's window was entrancing – I fluttered towards it like a moth. How would such a sour old creature be celebrating Christmas Eve? Thinking black thoughts, beside his embers, stroking his wicked one-eyed cat.

The snow crashed like thin fragile glass under my feet.

I stood at last outside the fisherman's window. I looked in.

What I saw was astonishing beyond ghosts or trows.

There was no crotchety old man inside, no one-eyed cat, no

ingrained filth and hung cobwebs. The paraffin lamp threw a circle of soft light, and all that was gathered inside that radiance was clean and pristine: the cups and plates on the dresser, the clock and ship-in-the-bottle and tea-caddies on the mantelpiece, the framed picture of Queen Victoria on the wall, the blue stones of the floor, the wood and straw of the fireside chair, the patchwork quilt on the bed.

A boy I had never seen before was sitting at the table. He might have been about my own age, and his head was a mass of bronze ringlets. On the table in front of him were an apple, an orange, a little sailing ship crudely cut from wood, with linen sails, probably cut from an old shirt. The boy – whoever he was – considered these objects with the utmost gravity. Once he put out his finger and touched the hull of the toy ship; as if it was so precious it had to be treated with special delicacy, lest it broke like a soap-bubble. I couldn't see the boy's face – only his bright hair, his lissom neck, and the gravity and joy that informed all his gestures. These were his meagre Christmas presents; silently he rejoiced in them.

Beyond the circle of lamp-light, were there other dwellers in the house? There may have been hidden breath in the darkened box bed in the corner.

I don't know how long I stood in the bitter night outside. My hands were trembling. I looked down at them – they were blue with cold.

Then, suddenly, for a second, the boy inside the house turned his face to the window. Perhaps he had heard the tiny splinterings of snow under my boots, or my quickened heart-beats.

The face that looked at me was Jock Scabra's, but Jock Scabra's from far back at the pure source of his life, sixty winters ago, before the ring was in his ear and before bad temper and perversity had grained black lines and furrows into his face. It was as if a cloth had been taken to a tarnished web-clogged mirror.

The boy turned back, smiling, to his Christmas hoard.

I turned and went home. I lifted the latch quietly, not to awaken Aunty Belle – for, if she knew what I had been up to that midnight, there would have been little of her 'spirit of generosity' for me. I crept, trembling, into bed.

When I woke up on Christmas morning, the 'spirit of the season' had loaded my stocking and the chair beside the bed with boxes of sweets, a Guinness Book of Records, a digital watch, a game of space wars, a cowboy hat, and a 50 pence piece. Aunty Belle stood at my bedroom door, smiling. And, 'A Merry Christmas,' she said.

Breakfast over, I couldn't wait to get back to the Scabra house. The village was taken over by children with apples, snowballs, laughter as bright as bells.

I peered in at the window. All was as it had been. The piratical old man sluiced the last of his breakfast tea down his throat from a cracked saucer. He fell to picking his black-and-yellow teeth with a kipper-bone. His house was like a midden.

The one-eyed cat yawned wickedly beside the new flames in the hearth.

JOHN EVELYN

from his *Diary*

1683

27th DECEMBER. I went to visit Sir John Chardin, a French gentleman, who travelled three times by land into Persia, and had made many curious researches in his travels, of which he was now setting forth a relation. It being in England this year one of the severest frosts that has happened of many years, he told me the cold in Persia was much greater, the ice of an incredible thickness; that they had little use of iron in all that country, it being so moist (though the air admirably clear and healthy) that oil would not preserve it from rusting, so that they had neither clocks nor watches; some padlocks they had for doors and boxes.

30th DECEMBER. Dr Sprat, now made Dean of Westminster, preached to the King at Whitehall, on Matt. vi. 24. Recollecting the passages of the past year, I gave God thanks for his mercies, praying his blessing for the future.

1684

1st JANUARY. The weather continuing intolerably severe, streets of booths were set upon the Thames; the air was so very cold and thick, as of many years there had not been the like. The small-pox was very mortal.

2nd JANUARY. I dined at Sir Stephen Fox's: after dinner came a fellow who ate live charcoal, glowingly ignited, quenching them in his mouth, and then champing and swallowing them down. There was a dog also which seemed to do many rational actions.

6th JANUARY. The river quite frozen.

9th JANUARY. I went across the Thames on the ice, now become so thick as to bear not only streets of booths, in which they roasted meat, and had divers shops of wares, quite across as in a town, but coaches, carts, and horses passed over. So I went from Westminster-stairs to Lambeth, and dined with the Archbishop: where I met my Lord Bruce, Sir George Wheler, Colonel Cooke, and several divines. After dinner and discourse with his Grace till evening prayers, Sir George Wheler and I walked over the ice from Lambeth-stairs to the Horse-ferry.

10th JANUARY. I visited Sir Robert Reading, where after supper we had music, but not comparable to that which Mrs Bridgeman made us on the guitar with such extraordinary skill and dexterity.

16th JANUARY. The Thames was filled with people and tents, selling all sorts of wares as in the city.

24th JANUARY. The frost continuing more and more severe, the Thames before London was still planted with booths in formal streets, all sorts of trades and shops furnished, and full of commodities, even to a printing-press, where the people and ladies took a fancy to have their names printed, and the day and year set down when printed on the Thames: this humour took so universally, that it was estimated that the printer gained £5 a day, for printing a line only, at sixpence a name, besides what he got by ballads, etc. Coaches plied from Westminster to the Temple, and from several other stairs to and fro, as in the streets, sleds, sliding with skates, a bull-baiting, horse and coach-races, puppet-plays and interludes, cooks, tippling, and other lewd places, so that it seemed to be a bacchanalian triumph, or carnival on the water, while it was a severe judgment on the land, the trees not only splitting as if lightning-struck, but men and cattle perishing in divers places, and the very seas so locked up with ice, that no vessels could stir out or come in. The fowls, fish, and birds, and all our exotic plants and greens, universally perishing. Many parks of deer were destroyed, and all sorts of fuel so dear, that there were great contributions to preserve the poor alive. Nor was this severe weather much less intense in most parts of Europe, even as far as Spain and the most southern tracts. London, by reason of the excessive coldness of the air hindering the ascent of the smoke, was so filled with the fuliginous steam of the sea-coal, that hardly could one see across the streets, and this filling the lungs with its gross particles, exceedingly obstructed the breast, so as one could scarcely breathe. Here was no water to be had from the pipes and engines, nor could the brewers and divers other tradesmen work, and every moment was full of disastrous accidents.

4th FEBRUARY. I went to Sayes Court to see how the frost had dealt with my garden, where I found many of the greens and rare plants utterly destroyed. The oranges and myrtles very sick, the rosemary and laurels dead to all appearance, but the cypress likely to endure it.

5th FEBRUARY. It began to thaw, but froze again. My coach crossed from Lambeth, to the Horse-ferry at Millbank, Westminster. The booths were almost all taken down; but there was first a map or landscape cut in copper representing all the manner of the camp, and the several actions, sports, and pastimes thereon, in memory of so signal a frost.

John Gay

from *Trivia: or,*
The Art of Walking the Streets of London

O roving Muse, recal that wond'rous year,
When winter reign'd in bleak *Britannia*'s air;
When hoary *Thames*, with frosted oziers crown'd,
Was three long moons in icy fetters bound.
The waterman, forlorn along the shore,
Pensive reclines upon his useless oar,
Sees harness'd steeds desert the stony town;
And wander roads unstable, not their own:
Wheels o'er the harden'd waters smoothly glide,
And rase with whiten'd tracks the slipp'ry tide.
Here the fat cook piles high the blazing fire,
And scarce the spit can turn the steer entire.
Booths sudden hide the *Thames*, long streets appear,
And num'rous games proclaim the crouded fair.
So when a general bids the martial train
Spread their encampment o'er the spacious plain;
Thick rising tents a canvas city build,
And the loud dice resound thro' all the field.

HENRY JAMES

from *English Hours*

I LEFT TOWN a short time before Christmas and went to spend the festive season in the North, in a part of the country with which I was unacquainted. It was quite possible to absent one's self from London without a sense of sacrifice, for the charms of the capital during the last several weeks have been obscured by peculiarly vile weather. It is of course a very old story that London is foggy, and this simple statement raises no blush on the face of Nature as we see it here. But there are fogs and fogs, and the folds of the black mantle have been during the present winter intolerably thick. The thickness that draws down and absorbs the smoke of the housetops, causes it to hang about the streets in impenetrable density, forces it into one's eyes and down one's throat, so that one is half blinded and quite sickened – this form of the particular plague has been much more frequent than usual. Just before Christmas, too, there was a heavy snowstorm, and even a tolerably light fall of snow has London quite at its mercy. The emblem of purity is almost immediately converted into a sticky, lead-coloured mush, the cabs skulk out of sight or take up their stations before the lurid windows of a public-house, which glares through the sleety darkness at the desperate wayfarer with an air of vulgar bravado. For recovery of one's nervous balance the only course was flight – flight to the country and the confinement of one's vision to the large area of one of those admirable homes which at this season overflow with hospitality and good cheer. By this means the readjustment is effectually brought about – these are conditions that you cordially appreciate. Of all the great things that the English have invented and made a part of the credit of the national character, the most perfect, the most characteristic, the one they have mastered most completely in all its details, so that it has become a compendious illustration of their social genius and their manners, is the well-appointed, well-administered, well-filled country-house. The grateful stranger makes these reflections – and others besides – as he wanders about in the beautiful library of such a dwelling, of an inclement winter afternoon, just at the hour when six o'clock tea is impending. Such a place and such a time abound in agreeable episodes; but I suspect that the episode from which, a fortnight ago, I received the most ineffaceable impression was but indirectly connected with the charms of a luxurious fireside. The country I speak of was a populous manufacturing region, full of tall chimneys and of an air that is gray and gritty. A lady had made a present of a Christmas-tree to the children of a workhouse, and she invited me to go with her and assist at the distribution of the toys. There was a drive through the early dusk of a very cold Christmas Eve, followed by the drawing up of a lamp-lit brougham in the snowy quadrangle of a grim-looking charitable institution. I had never been in an English workhouse before, and this one transported me, with the aid of memory, to the early pages of 'Oliver Twist'. We passed through cold, bleak passages, to which an odour of suet-pudding, the aroma of Christmas cheer, failed to impart an air of hospitality; and then, after waiting a while in a little parlour appertaining to the superintendent, where the remainder of a dinner of by no means eleemosynary simplicity and the attitude of a gentleman asleep with a flushed face on the sofa seemed to effect a tacit exchange of references, we were ushered into a large frigid refectory, chiefly illumined by the twinkling tapers of the Christmas-tree. Here entered to us some hundred and fifty little children of charity, who had been making a copious dinner and who brought with them an atmosphere of hunger memorably satisfied – together with other traces of the occasion upon their pinafores and their small red faces. I have said that the place reminded me of 'Oliver Twist', and I glanced through this little herd for an infant figure that should look as if it were cut out for romantic adventures. But they were all very prosaic little mortals. They were made of very common clay indeed, and a certain number of them were idiotic. They filed up and received their little offerings, and then they compressed themselves into a tight infantine bunch and, lifting up their small hoarse voices, directed a melancholy hymn toward their benefactress. The scene was a picture I shall not forget, with its curious mixture of poetry and sordid prose – the dying wintry light in the big, bare, stale room; the beautiful Lady Bountiful, standing in the twinkling glory of the Christmas-tree; the little multitude of staring and wondering, yet perfectly expressionless, faces.

WILLIAM SHAKESPEARE

from *As You Like It*

Blow, blow, thou winter wind.
Thou art not so unkind
As man's ingratitude;
Thy tooth is not so keen
Because thou art not seen,
Although thy breath be rude.
Heigh-ho! sing, heigh-ho! unto the green holly:
Most friendship is feigning, most loving mere folly:
Then, heigh-ho! the holly!
This life is most jolly.
Freeze, freeze, thou bitter sky,
Thou dost not bite so nigh
As benefits forgot:
Though thou the waters warp,
Thy sting is not so sharp
As friend remember'd not.
Heigh-ho! sing, heigh-ho! unto the green holly:
Most friendship is feigning, most loving mere folly:
Then, heigh-ho! the holly!
This life is most jolly.

Jane Austen

from *Emma*

Mr Woodhouse had so completely made up his mind to the visit, that in spite of the increasing coldness, he seemed to have no idea of shrinking from it, and set forward at last most punctually with his eldest daughter in his own carriage, with less apparent consciousness of the weather than either of the others; too full of the wonder of his own going, and the pleasure it was to afford at Randalls, to see that it was cold, and too well wrapt up to feel it. The cold, however, was severe; and by the time the second carriage was in motion, a few flakes of snow were finding their way down, and the sky had the appearance of being so overcharged as to want only a milder air to produce a very white world in a very short time.

Emma soon saw that her companion was not in the happiest humour. The preparing and the going abroad in such weather, with the sacrifice of his children after dinner, were evils, were disagreeables at least, which Mr John Knightley did not by any means like; he anticipated nothing in the visit that could be at all worth the purchase; and the whole of their drive to the vicarage was spent by him in expressing his discontent.

'A man,' said he, 'must have a very good opinion of himself when he asks people to leave their own fireside, and encounter such a day as this, for the sake of coming to see him. He must think himself a most agreeable fellow; I could not do such a thing. It is the greatest absurdity – actually snowing at this moment! The folly of not allowing people to be comfortable at home, and the folly of people's not staying comfortably at home when they can! If we were obliged to go out such an evening as this, by any call of duty or business, what a hardship we should deem it; – and here are we, probably with rather thinner clothing than usual, setting forward voluntarily, without excuse, in defiance of the voice of nature, which tells man, in every thing given to his view or his feelings, to stay at home himself, and keep all under shelter that he can; – here are we setting forward to spend five dull hours in another man's house, with nothing to say or to hear that was not said and heard yesterday, and may not be said and heard again tomorrow. Going in dismal weather, to return probably in worse; – four horses and four servants taken out for nothing but to convey five idle, shivering creatures into colder rooms and worse company than they might have had at home.'

Emma did not find herself equal to give the pleased assent, which no doubt he was in the habit of receiving, to emulate the 'Very true, my love', which must have been usually administered by his travelling companion; but she had resolution enough to refrain from making any answer at all. She could not be complying; she dreaded being quarrelsome; her heroism reached only to silence. She allowed him to talk, and arranged the glasses, and wrapped herself up, without opening her lips.

They arrived, the carriage turned, the step was let down, and Mr Elton, spruce, black, and smiling, was with them instantly...

'What an excellent device,' said he, 'the use of a sheep-skin for carriages. How very comfortable they make it; – impossible to feel cold with such precautions. The contrivances of modern days, indeed, have rendered a gentleman's carriage perfectly complete.

One is so fenced and guarded from the weather, that not a breath of air can find its way unpermitted. Weather becomes absolutely of no consequence. It is a very cold afternoon – but in this carriage we know nothing of the matter. Ha! snows a little I see.'

'Yes,' said John Knightley, 'and I think we shall have a good deal of it.'

'Christmas weather,' observed Mr Elton. 'Quite seasonable; and extremely fortunate we may think ourselves that it did not begin yesterday, and prevent this day's party, which it might very possibly have done, for Mr Woodhouse would hardly have ventured had there been much snow on the ground; but now it is of no consequence. This is quite the season indeed for friendly meetings. At Christmas everybody invites their friends about them, and people think little of even the worst weather. I was snowed up at a friend's house once for a week. Nothing could be pleasanter. I went for only one night, and could not get away till that very day sennight.'

Mr John Knightley looked as if he did not comprehend the pleasure, but said only, coolly –

'I cannot wish to be snowed up a week at Randalls.'

At another time Emma might have been amused, but she was too much astonished now at Mr Elton's spirits for other feelings. Harriet seemed quite forgotten in the expectation of a pleasant party.

'We are sure of excellent fires,' continued he, 'and everything in the greatest comfort. Charming people, Mr and Mrs Weston; – Mrs Weston indeed is much beyond praise, and he is exactly what one values, so hospitable, and so fond of society; – it will be a small party, but where small parties are select, they are, perhaps, the most agreeable of any. Mr Weston's dining-room does not accommodate more than ten comfortably; and for my part, I would rather, under such circumstances, fall short by two than exceed by two. I think you will agree with me, (turning with a soft air to Emma,) I think I shall certainly have your approbation, though Mr Knightley, perhaps, from being used to the large parties of London, may not quite enter into our feelings.'

'I know nothing of the large parties of London, sir – I never dine with anybody.'

'Indeed!' (in a tone of wonder and pity), 'I had no idea that the law had been so great a slavery. Well, sir, the time must come when you will be paid for all this, when you will have little labour and great enjoyment.'

'My first enjoyment,' replied John Knightley, as they passed through the sweep-gate, 'will be to find myself safe at Hartfield again.'

WILLIAM MAKEPEACE THACKERAY

The Mahogany Tree

Christmas is here:
Winds whistle shrill,
Icy and chill,
Little care we:
Little we fear
Weather without,
Sheltered about
The Mahogany Tree.

Once on the boughs
Birds of rare plume
Sang, in its bloom;
Night-birds are we:
Here we carouse,
Singing like them,
Perched round the stem
Of the jolly old tree.

Here let us sport,
Boys, as we sit;
Laughter and wit
Flashing so free.
Life is but short –
When we are gone,
Let them sing on
Round the old tree.

Evenings we knew,
Happy as this;
Faces we miss,
Pleasant to see.
Kind hearts and true,
Gentle and just,
Peace to your dust!
We sing round the tree.

Care, like a dun,
Lurks at the gate:
Let the dog wait;
Happy we'll be!
Drink, every one;
Pile up the coals,
Fill the red bowls,
Round the old tree!

Drain we the cup –
Friend, art afraid?
Spirits are laid
In the Red Sea.
Mantle it up;
Empty it yet;
Let us forget,
Round the old tree.

Sorrows, begone!
Life and its ills,
Duns and their bills,
Bid we to flee.
Come with the dawn,
Blue-devil sprite.
Leave us to-night,
Round the old tree.

CHARLES DICKENS

from *The Pickwick Papers*

WHILE MR PICKWICK was delivering himself of the sentiment just recorded, Mr Weller and the fat boy, having by their joint endeavours cut out a slide, were exercising themselves thereupon in a very masterly and brilliant manner. Sam Weller, in particular, was displaying that beautiful feat of fancy sliding, which is currently denominated 'knocking at the cobbler's door,' and which is achieved by skimming over the ice on one foot, and occasionally giving a postman's knock upon it with the other. It was a good long slide, and there was something in the motion which Mr Pickwick, who was very cold with standing still, could not help envying.

'It looks a nice warm exercise that, doesn't it?' he inquired of Wardle, when that gentleman was thoroughly out of breath, by reason of the indefatigable manner in which he had converted his legs into a pair of compasses, and drawn complicated problems on the ice.

'Ah, it does, indeed,' replied Wardle. 'Do you slide?'

'I used to do so, on the gutters, when I was a boy,' replied Mr Pickwick.

'Try it now,' said Wardle.

'Oh, do, please, Mr Pickwick!' cried all the ladies.

'I should be very happy to afford you any amusement,' replied Mr Pickwick, 'but I haven't done such a thing these thirty years.'

'Pooh! pooh! Nonsense!' said Wardle, dragging off his skates with the impetuosity which characterised all his proceedings.

'Here; I'll keep you company; come along!' And away went the good-tempered old fellow down the slide, with a rapidity which came very close upon Mr Weller, and beat the fat boy all to nothing.

Mr Pickwick paused, considered, pulled off his gloves and put them in his hat; took two or three short runs, baulked himself as often, and at last took another run, and went slowly and gravely down the slide, with his feet about a yard and a quarter apart, amidst the gratified shouts of all the spectators.

'Keep the pot a bilin', Sir!' said Sam; and down went Wardle again, and then Mr Pickwick, and then Sam, and then Mr Winkle, and then Mr Bob Sawyer, and then the fat boy, and then Mr Snodgrass, following closely upon each other's heels, and running after each other with as much eagerness as if all their future prospects in life depended on their expedition.

It was the most intensely interesting thing to observe the manner in which Mr Pickwick performed his share in the ceremony; to watch the torture of anxiety with which he viewed the person behind, gaining upon him at the imminent hazard of tripping him up; to see him gradually expend the painful force he had put on at first, and turn slowly round on the slide, with his face towards the point from which he had started; to contemplate the playful smile which mantled on his face when he had accomplished the distance, and the eagerness with which he turned round when he had done so, and ran after his predecessor, his black gaiters tripping pleasantly through the snow, and his eyes beaming cheerfulness and gladness through his spectacles. And when he was knocked down (which happened upon the average every third round), it was the most invigorating sight that can possibly be imagined, to behold him gather up his hat, gloves, and handkerchief, with a

A dozen shawls were offered on the instant. Three or four of the thickest having been selected, Mr Pickwick was wrapped up, and started off, under the guidance of Mr Weller; presenting the singular phenomenon of an elderly gentleman, dripping wet, and without a hat, with his arms bound down to his sides, skimming over the ground, without any clearly defined purpose, at the rate of six good English miles an hour.

But Mr Pickwick cared not for appearances in such an extreme case, and urged on by Sam Weller, he kept at the very top of his speed until he reached the door of Manor Farm, where Mr Tupman had arrived some five minutes before, and had frightened the old lady into palpitations of the heart by impressing her with the unalterable conviction that the kitchen chimney was on fire – a calamity which always presented itself in glowing colours to the old lady's mind when anybody about her evinced the smallest agitation.

Mr Pickwick paused not an instant until he was snug in bed. Sam Weller lighted a blazing fire in the room, and took up his dinner; a bowl of punch was carried up afterwards, and a grand carouse held in honour of his safety. Old Wardle would not hear of his rising, so they made the bed the chair, and Mr Pickwick presided. A second and a third bowl were ordered in; and when Mr Pickwick awoke next morning, there was not a symptom of rheumatism about him; which proves, as Mr Bob Sawyer very justly observed, that there is nothing like hot punch in such cases; and that if ever hot punch did fail to act as a preventive, it was merely because the patient fell into the vulgar error of not taking enough of it.

NEW YEAR

Percy Bysshe Shelley

Dirge for the Year

Orphan Hours, the year is dead,
　　Come and sigh, come and weep!
Merry Hours, smile instead,
　　For the Year is but asleep.
See, it smiles as it is sleeping,
Mocking your untimely weeping.

As an earthquake rocks a corse
　　In its coffin in the clay,
So White Winter, that rough nurse,
　　Rocks the death-cold Year to-day;
Solemn Hours! wail aloud
For your mother in her shroud.

As the wild air stirs and sways
　　The tree-swung cradle of a child,
So the breath of these rude days
　　Rocks the Year: – be calm and mild,
Trembling Hours; she will arise
With new love within her eyes.

January grey is here,
　　Like a sexton by her grave;
February bears the bier,
　　March with grief doth howl and rave,
And April weeps – but, O ye Hours,
Follow with May's fairest flowers.

1 January 1821

ROBERT HERRICK

Ceremony upon Candlemas Eve

Down with the Rosemary, and so
Down with the Baies, and misletoe;
Down with the Holly, Ivie, all,
Wherewith ye drest the Christmas Hall:
That so the superstitious find
No one least Branch there left behind:
For look, how many leaves there be
Neglected there, maids, trust to me,
So many Goblins you shall see.

Thomas Hood

Sonnet

Along the Woodford road there comes a noise
Of wheels, and Mr Rounding's neat postchaise
Struggles along, drawn by a pair of bays,
With Rev Mr Crow and six small Boys;
Who ever and anon declare their joys,
With trumping horns and juvenile huzzas,
At going home to spend their Christmas days,
And changing Learning's pains for Pleasure's toys.
Six weeks elapse, and down the Woodford way,
A heavy coach drags six more heavy souls,
But no glad urchins shout, no trumpets bray;
The carriage makes a halt, the gate-bell tolls,
And little Boys walk in as dull and mum
As six new scholars to the Deaf and Dumb.

Alfred Tennyson

Ring Out, Wild Bells
from *In Memoriam*

Ring out, wild bells, to the wild sky,
   The flying cloud, the frosty light:
   The year is dying in the night;
Ring out, wild bells, and let him die.

Ring out the old, ring in the new,
   Ring, happy bells, across the snow:
   The year is going, let him go;
Ring out the false, ring in the true.

Ring out the grief that saps the mind,
   For those that here we see no more;
   Ring out the feud of rich and poor,
Ring in redress to all mankind.

Ring out a slowly dying cause,
   And ancient forms of party strife;
   Ring in the nobler modes of life,
With sweeter manners, purer laws.

Ring out the want, the care the sin,
   The faithless coldness of the times;
   Ring out, ring out my mournful rhymes,
But ring the fuller minstrel in.

Alfred Tennyson

Ring Out, Wild Bells
from *In Memoriam*

Ring out, wild bells, to the wild sky,
  The flying cloud, the frosty light:
  The year is dying in the night;
Ring out, wild bells, and let him die.

Ring out the old, ring in the new,
  Ring, happy bells, across the snow:
  The year is going, let him go;
Ring out the false, ring in the true.

Ring out the grief that saps the mind,
  For those that here we see no more;
  Ring out the feud of rich and poor,
Ring in redress to all mankind.

Ring out a slowly dying cause,
  And ancient forms of party strife;
  Ring in the nobler modes of life,
With sweeter manners, purer laws.

Ring out the want, the care the sin,
  The faithless coldness of the times;
  Ring out, ring out my mournful rhymes,
But ring the fuller minstrel in.

Ring out false pride in place and blood,
  The civic slander and the spite;
  Ring in the love of truth and right,
Ring in the common love of good.

Ring out old shapes of foul disease;
  Ring out the narrowing lust of gold;
  Ring out the thousand wars of old,
Ring in the thousand years of peace.

Ring in the valiant man and free,
  The larger heart, the kindlier hand;
  Ring out the darkness of the land,
Ring in the Christ that is to be.

ALSO AVAILABLE AS A 2CD SET

Read by Juliet Stevenson and Simon Callow

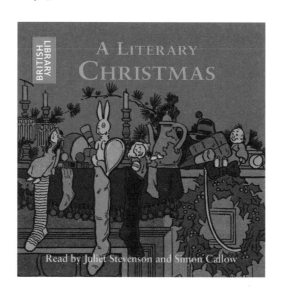

ISBN 978 0 7123 5130 0
2 CDs with booklet £12.99
Running time 138 minutes